SUPERFOODS

SUPERFOODS

The **50** Best Foods for You!

This edition published in 2012
LOVE FOOD is an imprint of Parragon Books Ltd

Parragon
Chartist House
15-17 Trim Street
Bath BA1 1HA, UK

ISBN: 978-1-4454-9506-4

Printed in China

Photography by Clive Streeter
Nutritional information by Judith Wills

Notes for the Reader
This book uses standard kitchen measuring spoons and cups. All spoon and cup measurements
are level unless otherwise indicated. Unless otherwise stated, milk is assumed to be whole,
eggs are large, individual vegetables are medium, and pepper is freshly ground black pepper.
Unless otherwise stated, all root vegetables should be washed and peeled before using.

For the best results, use a meat thermometer when cooking large cuts of meat and whole
poultry—check the latest USDA government guidelines for current advice.

Garnishes and serving suggestions are all optional and not necessarily included in the recipe
ingredients or method. The times given are only an approximate guide. Preparation times
differ according to the techniques used by different people and the cooking times may also
vary from those given. Optional ingredients, variations, or serving suggestions have not
been included in the calculations.

Recipes using raw or very lightly cooked eggs should be avoided by infants, the elderly,
pregnant women, and people with weakened immune systems. Pregnant and breast-feeding
women are advised to avoid eating peanuts and peanut products. People with nut allergies
should be aware that some of the prepared ingredients used in the recipes in this book
may contain nuts. Always check the packaging before use.

Picture acknowledgments
Close up of Raspberries, hindberries © TS Photography/Getty Images
Bunches of bananas (full frame) © Lottie Davies/Getty Images
Blueberries © Daniel Hurst Photography/Getty Images
Peas, close-up © Robin MacDougall/Getty Images
Carrots with tops, close-up ©) Foodcollection RF/Getty Images

Contents

Introduction

If you want to live a long and healthy life, there are many simple lifestyle changes that can boost both your brain and body functions. Most experts agree that the secret to a healthy lifestyle requires just a little common sense— clean living, eating a balanced diet, and getting plenty of exercise are all important. Choosing a healthy diet that is rich in superfoods is an easy step to improving how you look and feel.

What is a superfood?

The theory that certain foods can have a lasting effect on our health and well-being is certainly not a new one. More than two thousand years ago the father of modern medicine, Hippocrates, wrote about the link between diet and health, and modern-day physicians and dietitians are increasingly looking to our diet and so-called superfoods to help prevent and treat a whole host of diseases, including cancer, heart disease, Alzheimer's, stroke, cataracts, and many others.

All foods have some nutritional value, but superfoods earn their name because they contain particularly high levels of a particular vitamin, mineral, essential fatty acid, or phytochemical that has been shown to improve some aspect of our health or well-being.

Superfoods come in all shapes and sizes, but the best way to be sure that you get a good selection is to make plant-based foods—such as fruit and vegetables, whole-grain cereals, beans, nuts, and seeds—the dominant ingredients in your diet.

In the pages that follow, you will find a whole host of so-called superfoods that are readily available, easy to prepare, and make a delicious addition to your usual diet. Each page details the nutritional benefits that can be found in a particular ingredient, along with information on how best to prepare and store certain foods.

Superfood facts

• Some superfoods, such as blueberries, red bell pepper, and oranges, have vitamins and antioxidants that help reduce damage to cells.

• Green leafy vegetables, such as broccoli, kale, and watercress, contain naturally occurring plant chemicals, called phytochemicals, which work to block the growth of cancerous cells.

• Others, such as garlic and onions, earn their superfood status because they actively help to strengthen the immune system by boosting the body's natural resistance to disease and infection.

- Oil-rich fish, such as salmon, fresh tuna, mackerel, and sardines, offer a wealth of health benefits. The omega-3 fats found in these fish help to keep the heart healthy and also have an anti-inflammatory effect, which can help to relieve the symptoms associated with such conditions as rheumatoid arthritis.

- Studies have also shown that regular inclusion of oily fish in the diet can help improve concentration for both children and adults—and although they won't actually make you smarter, as many people believe, they certainly have a beneficial effect on mental focus and productive output.

- Many herbs and spices have superfood qualities. Cinnamon for instance, which is a key ingredient in many sweet recipes, is believed to help lower bad cholesterol and improve blood sugar levels in the blood. It also has anti-inflammatory and antibacterial properties that help to fight infection in the body.

Choosing superfoods

The good news is that, despite their incredible health-boosting properties, superfoods don't have to be expensive or exotic—many of the fruits and vegetables we consume every day, such as carrots, beets, apples, lentils,

and tomatoes, contain compounds that technically make them superfoods. Put simply, this means that making the change to a healthy, balanced diet doesn't have to be expensive, and doesn't require hunting in health food stores for unusual ingredients—just include more of the good stuff!

The theory that eating certain foods can help you live a longer and healthier life has been supported by a growing body of evidence from around the world. Some studies suggest that the right diet may even help counteract the negative effects of smoking, lack of exercise, and the stresses of modern

living, and that certain foods could be the answer to niggling health problems such as indigestion, headaches, and lack of energy. It might seem as though the easy alternative to a diet overhaul is to take a vitamin pill every morning, but it's important to remember that most superfoods contain a cocktail of active ingredients and it's this combination (and interaction) that offer the health benefits.

In this book, we'll give you the lowdown on the top 50 everyday superfoods for you—and show you how to supercharge your diet with quick, easy, and delicious recipes packed full of goodness!

01

Apples

In recent years, scientific evidence has shown that the old health proverb—an apple a day keeps the doctor away—may, in fact, be correct.

MAJOR NUTRIENTS PER AVERAGE APPLE

Calories	60
Total fat	Trace
Protein	Trace
Carbohydrate	16 g
Fiber	2.8 g
Vitamin C	5 mg
Potassium	123 mg

Although apples don't, with the exception of potassium, contain standout amounts of any particular vitamin or mineral, they do contain high levels of various plant chemicals, including the flavonoid quercetin. This is effective in protecting the body against a wide variety of diseases, including cancer and Alzheimer's, and it also has anti-inflammatory properties. Apples are a valuable source of pectin, a soluble fiber that can help to lower bad cholesterol (which can slowly build up in the inner walls of the arteries that feed the heart and brain) and help prevent colon cancer. Research has found that adults who regularly eat apples have smaller waistlines, less abdominal fat, and lower blood pressure than those who don't.

• Rich in flavonoids for healthy heart and lungs.
• Low in calories and low on the glycemic index (GI).
• High fiber content that is good for digestion.
• A good source of potassium, which can prevent fluid retention.

Practical tips:
Keep apples in a dark, cool place, such as your refrigerator, or a cupboard—they should be stored in a plastic bag with air holes, in order to retain maximum amounts of their vitamin C content. To prevent browning, place cut slices into a bowl of water with 1–2 tablespoons of lemon juice. Always try to eat the skin because it contains up to five times as many plant chemicals as the flesh.

Stuffed baked apples

SERVES 4

3 tablespoons blanched almonds
½ cup plumped dried apricots
1 piece preserved ginger, drained
1 tablespoon honey
1 tablespoon syrup from the preserved ginger jar
¼ cup rolled oats
4 large Granny Smith or other cooking apples

METHOD

1 Preheat the oven to 350°F. Using a sharp knife, finely chop the almonds, apricots, and preserved ginger. Set aside until needed.

2 Place the honey and syrup in a saucepan and heat until the honey has melted. Stir in the oats and cook gently over low heat for 2 minutes. Remove the saucepan from the heat and stir in the almonds, apricots, and preserved ginger.

3 Core the apples, widen the tops slightly, and score horizontally around the circumference of each to prevent the skins from bursting during cooking.

4 Place the apples in an ovenproof dish and fill the cavities with the stuffing. Pour water into the dish until it comes about one-third of the way up the apples. Bake in the preheated oven for 40 minutes, or until tender. Serve immediately.

02

Avocados

The buttery green flesh of the avocado is a rich source of monounsaturated fats, which are important for a healthy heart, and is packed with other important nutrients.

Avocados are high in fat, but this fat is mostly monounsaturated, which can, in fact, help to reduce bad blood cholesterol levels. The oleic acid contained in monounsaturates has also been linked with a lower risk of breast cancer. Avocados boast a large range of other nutrients, including vitamins C, E, and B6, folate, iron, magnesium, and potassium. They also contain the antioxidant plant chemical beta-sitosterol, which has been shown to improve blood cholesterol levels, help to prevent cancer, and has even been linked to improving age-related male hair loss.

- High vitamin E content boosts the immune system.
- Lutein helps protect against eye cataracts and age-related degeneration of the retina.
- High monounsaturated fat helps lower cholesterol.
- Good source of magnesium for a healthy heart.

Practical tips:
Choose avocados that have unblemished skins without soft spots, which suggest bruising. They're ready to eat if the flesh yields slightly when pressed with the thumb. To hasten ripening, put them in a paper bag with a banana. To prepare, cut lengthwise down to the pit and twist to separate the two halves. Pierce the pit with the tip of a knife, then pull to remove. Once cut, use lemon juice or vinegar to prevent discoloration.

MAJOR NUTRIENTS PER AVERAGE AVOCADO

Calories	240
Total fat	3 g
Protein	22 g
Carbohydrate	12.8 g
Fiber	5 g
Vitamin C	9 mg
Potassium	728 mg
Vitamin E	3 mg

Spicy avocado dip

SERVES 4

2 large avocados
juice of 1–2 limes
2 large garlic cloves, crushed
1 teaspoon mild chili powder,
or to taste
salt and pepper

METHOD

1 Cut the avocados in half. Remove the pits and discard. Scoop out the flesh and discard the skins.

2 Place the avocado flesh in a food processor with the juice of 1 or 2 limes, according to taste. Add the garlic and chili powder and process until smooth.

3 Transfer to a serving bowl, season with salt and pepper, and serve.

03

Oranges

Vitamin C, the antioxidant vitamin that boosts the immune system and protects from the signs of ageing, is found in abundance in oranges.

Oranges are one of the least expensive sources of vitamin C, which protects against cell damage and disease. The fruit is also a good source of fiber, folate, and potassium as well as calcium, which is vital for bone maintenance. They contain the carotenes zeaxanthin and lutein, both of which can help to maintain eye health and protect against degeneration of the retina. Oranges also contain rutin, a flavonoid that can help slow down or prevent the growth of tumors, and nobiletin, an anti-inflammatory compound. All these plant compounds also help the vitamin C in oranges to work more effectively.

- High levels of vitamin C, which helps to prevent infections and reduce the severity and duration of colds.
- Low on the glycemic index (GI), so a useful fruit for dieters and diabetics.
- Good content of soluble fiber pectin, which helps control blood cholesterol levels.
- Anti-inflammatory, so may help reduce incidence of arthritis.

Practical tips:
Buy oranges that feel heavy to hold compared with their size—this means they should be juicy and fresh. Store them in the refrigerator to retain their vitamin C content. Orange peel contains high levels of nutrients, but should be scrubbed and dried before use.

MAJOR NUTRIENTS PER AVERAGE ORANGE

Calories	65
Total fat	Trace
Protein	1 g
Carbohydrate	16 g
Fiber	3.4 g
Vitamin C	64 mg
Potassium	238 mg
Calcium	61 mg
Lutein/Zeaxanthin	182 mcg

Did you know?

You should eat some of the white pith of the orange, as well as the juicy flesh, because it contains high levels of fiber, useful plant chemicals, and antioxidants.

Orange & carrot stir-fry

SERVES 4

2 tablespoons peanut oil

8 carrots, shredded

2½ leeks, thinly sliced

2 oranges, peeled and segmented

2 tablespoons ketchup

1 tablespoon demerara sugar
or other raw sugar

2 tablespoons light soy sauce

½ cup chopped peanuts

METHOD

1 Heat a wok or skillet over high heat. Add the oil and heat for
   30 seconds. Add the shredded carrots and sliced leeks and
   stir-fry for 2–3 minutes, or until the vegetables are just soft.

2 Add the orange segments to the wok and heat through gently.

3 Mix together the ketchup, sugar, and soy sauce in a small bowl.
   Add the mixture to the wok and stir-fry for 2 minutes.

4 Transfer the stir-fry to four warm serving bowls and sprinkle
   with the chopped peanuts. Serve immediately.

04

Grapefruit

The perfect healthy breakfast, the grapefruit, like many other citrus fruits, is an excellent source of vitamin C, which boosts the immune system.

In recent years, the pink-fleshed grapefruit has become as popular as the white or yellow-fleshed variety. It is a little sweeter and contains more health benefits—the pink pigment indicates the presence of lycopene, which has been shown to help prevent prostate and other cancers. Like other citrus fruits, the grapefruit contain bioflavonoids—compounds that appear to increase the benefits of vitamin C, which is also found in this fruit in excellent amounts. The grapefruit is low on the glycemic index (GI) and low in calories, so it is an important fruit for dieters. Because grapefruit juice can alter the effect of certain prescription medicines (such as those that lower blood pressure), people on medication should check with their physicians before they consume the fruit.

MAJOR NUTRIENTS PER HALF PINK GRAPEFRUIT

Calories	30
Total fat	Trace
Protein	0.5 g
Carbohydrate	7.5 g
Fiber	1.1 g
Vitamin C	37 mg
Potassium	127 mg
Beta-carotene	770 mcg
Folate	9 mcg
Calcium	15 mg

• High in antioxidants, which can help prevent prostate and other cancers.
• Rich in vitamin C to boost the immune system.
• Excellent fruit for dieters.

Did you know?

The slightly bitter taste of some grapefruit is caused by a compound known as naringenin, which has cholesterol-lowering properties.

Practical tips:
Grapefruit is delicious halved, sprinkled with demerara sugar or other raw sugar, and broiled for a short while, and makes the perfect healthy breakfast. Always try to eat some of the white pith with your grapefruit, because this is also high in nutrients. Grapefruit, like all citrus fruits, will contain more juice if they feel heavy in relation to their size.

Grapefruit & orange salad

SERVES 4

1 pink grapefruit
1 yellow grapefruit
3 oranges

METHOD

1 Using a sharp knife, carefully cut away all the peel from the grapefruit and oranges.

2 Working over a bowl to catch the juices, carefully cut the grapefruit and orange segments between the membranes to obtain skinless segments of fruit. Discard any seeds.

3 Add the segments to the bowl and gently mix together. Cover and let chill in the refrigerator until required, or serve immediately.

Kiwifruit

The "kiwi" has an unusual amount of omega-3 oils for a fruit. This, combined with its high vitamin C content, helps maintain healthy heart function.

Eating the edible seeds of fruits is extremely beneficial, and the seeds of the kiwi are particularly easy to swallow. As well as fiber and zinc, seeds contain all the nutrients and enzymes needed for a plant to grow, and when ingested they allow the body's cells to grow and regenerate. Kiwi seeds contain on average of 62 percent alpha linoleic acid, the omega-3 oil that helps protect the heart and decrease inflammation, both inside and outside the body. The kiwi is also a good source of copper, which is needed for collagen production and, therefore, healthy skin, nails, and muscles.

- High potassium content, which helps keep kidneys healthy.
- Contain more vitamin C than oranges, as well as vitamin E and rehydrating omega-3 oils for a skin-nourishing combination.
- Vitamin C works with copper to produce collagen, to keep skin renewed and firm.

Practical tips:
The kiwi can be eaten whole like an apple—eating the skin means you consume the vitamin C that lies just beneath it, and it vastly increases your intake of the fruit's insoluble fiber and antioxidant content. To test if a kiwi is ripe, press it—you should be able to depress the skin slightly, but the flesh beneath should be firm. Dried kiwi slices make healthy snacks, and can be bought in health food stores.

MAJOR NUTRIENTS PER AVERAGE KIWIFRUIT

Calories	46
Total fat	0.39 g
Protein	0.85 g
Carbohydrate	11.06 g
Fiber	2.26 g
Vitamin C	69.9 mg
Vitamin E	1.10 mg
Potassium	235 mg
Copper/Zeaxanthin	0.10 mcg
Calcium	22.66 mg
Zinc	25.64 mg
Omega-3 oils	31.75 mg

Kiwi smoothie

SERVES 2

1 mango
4 kiwis
1½ cups pineapple juice
4 fresh mint leaves

METHOD

1 Cut the mango into two thick slices, as close to the pit as possible. Scoop out the flesh and coarsely chop. Cut off any additional flesh adhering to the pit.
2 Peel the kiwis with a sharp knife and chop the flesh.
3 Put the mango, kiwis, pineapple juice, and mint leaves into a food processor or blender and process until thoroughly combined. Pour into chilled glasses and serve.

06

Blueberries

These deep purple berries are the richest of all fruits in antioxidant compounds, which could help to protect the body from various diseases.

Calories	29
Total fat	Trace
Protein	0.4 g
Carbohydrate	7.2 g
Fiber	1.2 g
Vitamin C	5 mg
Vitamin E	2.4 mg
Folate	34 mcg
Potassium	39 mg
Lutein/Zeaxanthin	40 mcg

The blueberry was one of the first fruits to be named a superfood, and it's thought that just a handful of berries a day could offer protection from some diseases. The compound pterostilbene, which is found in the fruit, could be as effective as commercial medicines in lowering cholesterol, and may also help prevent diabetes and some cancers. Blueberries are also a good source of anthocyanins, which can help to prevent heart disease and memory loss. They are high in vitamin C and fiber and also appear to help urinary tract infections.

• Contain a cholesterol-lowering compound.
• Can help prevent coronary heart disease, diabetes, and some cancers.
• Could help to treat urinary tract infections.
• Lutein and zeaxanthin helps keep eyes healthy.

Practical tips:
Blueberries are sweet and ideally should be eaten raw, which helps to preserve their vitamin C content. Store in a nonmetallic container, because contact with metal can discolor them. Blueberries are a valuable kitchen staple and can boost the nutrient content of muffins, cakes, crisps, pies, and fruit salads. The berries freeze well and lose few of their nutrients in the process.

Blueberry breakfast medley

SERVES 4

3 tablespoons honey
½ cup mixed unsalted nuts
½ cup low-fat Greek yogurt
1 ⅓ cups fresh blueberries

METHOD

1 Heat the honey in a small saucepan over medium heat. Add the nuts and stir until they are well coated. Remove from the heat and let cool slightly.

2 Divide the yogurt among four serving bowls, then spoon the nut mixture and blueberries over it and serve immediately.

Raspberries

Packed with vitamin C, fiber, and antioxidants to protect the heart, raspberries are one of the most nutritious fruits.

Raspberries are a surprisingly nutritious fruit, best eaten raw, because cooking or processing destroys some of the antioxidants, especially anthocyanins. Anthocyanins are naturally occurring red and purple pigments that have been shown to help prevent both heart disease and certain cancers, and may also help to prevent varicose veins. Raspberries also contain high levels of ellagic acid, a compound with anticancer properties. In addition, they are high in fiber and contain good amounts of iron, which the body absorbs well because of the accompanying high levels of vitamin C.

- High antioxidant content.
- May help to prevent varicose veins.
- One portion contains approximately half a day's recommended intake of vitamin C.
- High fiber content helps lower bad cholesterol.

MAJOR NUTRIENTS PER ¾ CUP/3½ OZ. RASPBERRIES

Calories	52
Total fat	0.6 g
Protein	1.2 g
Carbohydrate	12 g
Fiber	6.5 g
Vitamin C	26 mg
Vitamin B$_3$	0.6 mg
Vitamin E	0.8 mg
Folate	21 mcg
Potassium	151 mg
Calcium	25 mg
Iron	0.7 mg
Zinc	0.4 mg

Did you know?

Raspberries consist of smaller fruits called drupelets, which are clustered around a stalk core in the center. Each drupelet contains a seed, which is why raspberries are so high in fiber.

Practical tips:
Raspberries do not stay fresh for long, so should be picked only when ripe and need to be consumed relatively quickly. They do, however, freeze well, but they should be packed in single layers in plastic containers, not in plastic bags. Never wash raspberries before storing unless absolutely necessary—their structure is easily destroyed. The healthy soluble fiber in raspberries is pectin, which means they make excellent, easy-to-set preserves.

Raspberry & pear refresher

SERVES 2

2 large, ripe Bartlett pears
1 cup frozen raspberries
1 cup ice-cold water
honey, to taste
fresh raspberries, for
decorating (optional)

METHOD

1. Peel and quarter the pears, removing the cores. Place the pears in a food processor or blender with the raspberries and water and process until smooth.

2. Taste and sweeten with honey to taste. Pour into chilled glasses, decorate with raspberries, if using, and serve.

08

Bananas

The banana is the ultimate sports snack because it provides quick, quality fuel for the body. It is perfect for replenishing and repairing flagging cells.

Bananas are high in sugar, but they shouldn't be underestimated for their health-giving properties. A ripe banana contains a high amount of fiber, including the prebiotic inulin, which feeds our beneficial (probiotic) digestive bacteria, the first line of defense for the immune system. Keeping your digestive bacteria healthy can help prevent inflammatory conditions, such as eczema, asthma, and arthritis, and support the digestion and absorption of nutrients needed to maintain optimal health.

- Potassium and vitamin C help transport oxygen around the body to renew and revitalize the skin.
- Contain high levels of potassium, vitamin C and vitamin B_6, which are all important for heart health.
- Athletes draw on the rich nutritional mixture in bananas to support performance, recovery, and muscle response.
- Shown to help kidney function and eliminate fluid retention, reducing puffiness for a more youthful appearance.

Practical tips:
The fruit of choice for many people with a sweet tooth, bananas are best eaten when the skin is a solid yellow color, with no bruises. Avoid overripe, brown bananas because, by this stage, the sugars will have broken down and the fruit becomes soft and sweet. Bananas may not be suitable for people with phlegm and nasal congestion, because they can make these conditions worse.

MAJOR NUTRIENTS PER AVERAGE BANANA

Calories	105
Total fat	0.39 g
Protein	1.29 g
Carbohydrate	26.95 g
Fiber	3.1 g
Vitamin B_6	0.43 mg
Vitamin C	10.3 mg
Potassium	422 mg

Did you know?

The name banana comes from the Arabic *banan,* or "finger"; they grow in clusters of up to 20 fruit called a "hand."

Banana & strawberry smoothie

SERVES 2

1 banana, sliced

4 ounces strawberries, hulled

⅔ cup plain yogurt with live cultures

METHOD

1 Put the banana, strawberries, and yogurt into a food processor or blender and process for a few seconds until smooth. Pour into glasses and serve immediately.

09

Broccoli

Of all the vegetables in the brassica (cabbage) family, broccoli, with its high levels of selenium, has shown the highest levels of protection against prostate cancer.

Broccoli comes in several varieties, but the darker the color, the more beneficial nutrients the vegetable contains. It contains sulforaphane and indoles, which have been shown to help prevent cancer, particularly in the breast and colon. Broccoli is also high in flavonoids, which have been specifically linked with a significant reduction in the risk of ovarian cancer. The chemicals in broccoli are also thought to protect against stomach ulcers. They act as a detoxifier, helping to lower bad blood cholesterol, boost the immune system, and protect against cataracts.

- Rich in a variety of nutrients that protect against types of cancer.
- Lutein and zeaxanthin help prevent macular degeneration.
- Helps eradicate the *H. pylori* bacteria, encouraging a healthy digestive tract.
- High calcium content helps build and protect bones.
- Excellent source of the antioxidants vitamin C and selenium.

Practical tips:
Look for broccoli heads that are rich in color and avoid any with pale, yellow, or brown patches on the florets. You can eat the leaves and stems of broccoli, which are also nutritionally beneficial. Frozen broccoli contains all the nutrients of fresh broccoli, and offers a more convenient storage method. Cook by lightly steaming or stir-frying.

MAJOR NUTRIENTS PER 1 CUP/ 3½ OZ. CHOPPED BROCCOLI

Calories	34
Total fat	0.4 g
Protein	2.8 g
Carbohydrate	6.6 g
Fiber	2.6 g
Vitamin C	89 mg
Selenium	2.5 mcg
Beta-carotene	361 mcg
Calcium	47 mg
Lutein/Zeaxanthin	1,403 mcg

Broccoli & peanut stir-fry

SERVES 4

3 tablespoons vegetable oil or peanut oil

1 lemongrass stalk, coarsely chopped

2 fresh red chiles, seeded and chopped

1-inch piece fresh ginger, peeled and grated

3 kaffir lime leaves, coarsely torn

3 tablespoons Thai green curry paste

1 onion, chopped

1 red bell pepper, seeded and chopped

5 cups broccoli florets

1 cup trimmed beans

⅓ cup toasted unsalted peanuts

METHOD

1   Place 2 tablespoons of the oil, the lemongrass, chiles, ginger, lime leaves, and curry paste in a food processor or blender and process until a paste forms.

2   Heat a wok or skillet over high heat. Add the remaining oil and heat for 30 seconds. Add the spice paste, onion, and red bell pepper and stir-fry for 2–3 minutes, until the vegetables start to soften.

3   Add the broccoli and beans, cover, and cook over low heat for 4–5 minutes, until tender.

4   Add the peanuts to the wok, toss to mix, and serve.

10

Carrots

The richest in carotenes of all plant foods, carrots offer protection from cancers and cardiovascular disease, and they help keep eyes and lungs healthy.

Carrots are one of the most nutritious root vegetables. They are an excellent source of antioxidant compounds and the richest vegetable source of carotenes, which give them their bright orange color. These compounds help protect against cardiovascular disease and cancer. Carotenes may reduce the risk of heart disease by about 45 percent, promote good vision, and help maintain healthy lungs. They are also rich in fiber, antioxidant vitamins C and E, calcium, and potassium. There is ongoing research into the effect of falcarinol, a chemical in carrots, in suppressing tumors.

- High carotene content protects against high blood cholesterol and heart disease.
- May offer protection against some cancers and emphysema.
- Women who eat at least five carrots a week are nearly two-thirds less likely to have a stroke than those who don't.
- Help to protect sight and night vision.
- Contain a good range of vitamins, minerals, and fiber.

Practical tips:
The darker orange the carrot, the more carotenes it will contain. Remove any green on the stem end of the carrot before cooking, because it can be mildly toxic. The nutrients in carrots are more available to the body when a carrot is cooked, compared to when eaten raw, and adding a little vegetable oil during cooking helps the carotenes to be absorbed.

MAJOR NUTRIENTS PER AVERAGE CARROT

Calories	41
Total fat	Trace
Protein	0.9 g
Carbohydrate	9.6 g
Fiber	2.8 g
Vitamin C	6 mg
Vitamin E	0.7 mg
Beta-carotene	8,285 mcg
Calcium	33 mg
Potassium	320 mg
Lutein/Zeaxanthin	256 mcg

Did you know?

A very high intake of carrots can cause the skin to appear orange—called carotanemia, it is a harmless condition.

Carrot salad

SERVES 4-6

6 carrots (about 1 pound), peeled

1 tablespoon vegetable oil or peanut oil

½ tablespoon black mustard seeds

½ tablespoon cumin seeds

1 fresh green chile, seeded and finely chopped

½ teaspoon sugar

½ teaspoon salt

pinch of ground turmeric

1½–2 tablespoons lemon juice

METHOD

1 Coarsely shred the carrots into a bowl and set aside.

2 Heat a wok or skillet over medium–high heat. Add the oil and heat for 30 seconds. Add the mustard and cumin seeds and heat, stirring, until the mustard seeds start popping. Immediately remove the wok from the heat and stir in the chile, sugar, salt, and turmeric. Let cool for 5 minutes.

3 Pour the warm spices and any oil over the carrots and add the lemon juice. Toss together and adjust the seasoning, if necessary, then cover and chill in the refrigerator for at least 30 minutes. Toss to mix just before serving.

Red bell peppers

All members of the capsicum family, which includes chile and paprika, have fantastic youth-preserving benefits, and are especially good for the heart and skin.

The color of red bell peppers comes from the antioxidant carotenoid lycopene, just one of the nutrients that distinguishes them from green bell peppers. They also contain twice the amount of vitamin C and around nine times the carotene as their green counterparts. An important part of the youth-preserving Mediterranean diet, red bell peppers contribute to heart health, because their high levels of antioxidants keep the arteries in good condition. The vitamin B_6 and folate present also help to reduce levels of homocysteine, a substance we produce naturally but that is linked to heart disease and dementia if levels become high.

- Rich source of a range of vitamins, minerals, and plant chemicals.
- Vitamin A stops the damage to skin from UV light that can be seen as wrinkles and age spots.
- Vitamin C and vitamin B_6, which is needed to make stomach acid, vital for killing off harmful bacteria.
- Contain folate, needed for cell growth and skin renewal.

Practical tip:
A bell pepper should feel weighty and have a healthy green stem. The skin should be smooth, firm, and wrinkle-free. Avoid bell peppers with indents or black spots. Store, unwashed, in a plastic bag in the refrigerator for up to a week. Fat-soluble carotenoids need oil to carry them into the body, so eating red bell peppers with olive oil will double their health value and optimize their absorption by the body.

MAJOR NUTRIENTS PER AVERAGE RED BELL PEPPER

Calories	37
Total fat	0.36 g
Protein	1.18 g
Carbohydrate	7.18 g
Fiber	2.5 g
Vitamin A	6,681 IU
Vitamin C	222 mg
Vitamin B_6	0.35 mg
Folate	25.7 mcg

Stuffed red peppers with basil

SERVES 4

¾ cup long-grain brown rice

4 large red bell peppers

2 tablespoons olive oil

1 garlic clove, chopped

4 shallots, chopped

1 celery stalk, chopped

3 tablespoons chopped walnuts

2 tomatoes, peeled and chopped

1 tablespoon lemon juice

⅓ cup raisins

¼ cup freshly shredded cheddar cheese (optional)

2 tablespoons chopped fresh basil

salt and pepper

METHOD

1 Preheat the oven to 350°F. Cook the rice in a saucepan of lightly salted boiling water for 35 minutes. Drain, rinse under cold running water, then drain again.

2 Meanwhile, using a sharp knife, cut the tops off the bell peppers and reserve. Remove the seeds and white cores, then blanch the peppers and reserved tops in a saucepan of boiling water for 2 minutes. Drain and rinse under cold running water.

3 Heat half the oil in a large skillet. Add the garlic and shallots and cook, stirring, for 3 minutes. Add the celery, walnuts, tomatoes, lemon juice, and raisins and cook for an additional 5 minutes. Remove from the heat and stir in the rice, cheese, if using, chopped basil, and seasoning.

4 Stuff the peppers with the rice mixture and place in an ovenproof dish. Replace the tops on the peppers, drizzle with the remaining oil, loosely cover with aluminum foil, and bake in the preheated oven for 45 minutes. Remove from the oven and serve.

12

Brussels sprouts

Brussels sprouts are packed with immune-boosting nutrients, and they should be consumed regularly to enjoy the potential health benefits.

Brussels sprouts are an important winter vegetable, providing high levels of vitamin C and many other immune-boosting nutrients. They are rich in the sulforaphane compound, which is a detoxifier and has been shown to help the body clear itself of potential carcinogens. Brussels sprouts have been shown to help prevent DNA damage when eaten regularly and may help minimize the spread of breast cancer. They even contain small amounts of beneficial omega-3 fats, zinc, and selenium, a mineral many adults do not eat in the recommended daily amount. People who eat large quantities of Brussels sprouts and other brassicas (cabbage family vegetables) are thought to have a much lower risk of prostate, colorectal, and lung cancers.

- Rich in indoles and other compounds to protect against cancer, sprouts may also reduce the spread of cancer.
- Extremely rich in immune-boosting vitamin C.
- Indole content can also help lower bad blood cholesterol.
- Very high in fiber, which is good for digestive health.

Practical tips:
Select bright green sprouts with tight heads and no sign of yellow leaves. Lightly steaming or quickly boiling Brussels sprouts is the best way to cook them and preserve their nutrients. Don't overcook because much of the vitamin C content will be destroyed. Overcooking also alters their flavor and gives them an unwelcome odor.

MAJOR NUTRIENTS PER 5 BRUSSELS SPROUTS

Calories	43
Total fat	0.3 g
Protein	3.4 g
Carbohydrate	9 g
Fiber	3.8 g
Vitamin C	85 mg
Folate	61 mcg
Magnesium	23 mg
Calcium	42 mg
Selenium	1.6 mcg
Zinc	0.4 mg
Beta-carotene	450 mcg
Lutein/Zeaxanthin	1,590 mcg

Brussels sprouts with chestnuts

SERVES 4

4 cups Brussels sprouts, trimmed

2 tablespoons butter

1 cup canned shelled, whole chestnuts, drained

pinch of grated nutmeg

salt and pepper

½ cup slivered almonds, to garnish

METHOD

1 Cook the Brussels sprouts in a large saucepan of lightly salted, boiling water for 5 minutes. Drain thoroughly.

2 Melt the butter in a large saucepan over medium heat. Add the Brussels sprouts and sauté, stirring, for 3 minutes, then add the chestnuts and nutmeg.

3 Season with salt and pepper and stir well. Cook for an additional 2 minutes, then remove from the heat. Transfer to a warm dish, scatter with the almonds, and serve.

13

Tomatoes

The tomato is one of the healthiest foods because it contains lycopene, which offers protection from prostate cancer, and compounds to help prevent blood clots.

Tomatoes are our major source of dietary lycopene, a carotene antioxidant that fights heart disease and may help to prevent prostate cancer. Tomatoes also have an anticoagulant effect because of the salicylates contained in them, and they contain several other antioxidants including vitamin C, quercetin, and lutein. Tomatoes are low in calories but high in potassium, and contain useful amounts of fiber.

- Rich source of lycopene, which helps prevent prostate cancer.
- One medium tomato contains nearly one-quarter of the day's recommended intake of vitamin C for an adult.
- Rich in potassium to help regulate body fluids.
- Quercetin and lutein content helps to prevent cataracts and keep heart and eyes healthy.
- Contain salicylates, which have an anticoagulant effect.

Practical tips:
The more red and ripe the tomato is, the higher the levels of lycopene contained within. Vine-ripened tomatoes also contain more lycopene than those ripened after picking. The tomato peel is richer in nutrients than the flesh and the seed part in the center is high in salicylates, so for maximum nutritional benefits, avoid peeling and don't seed unless necessary. The lycopene in raw or cooked tomatoes is better absorbed in your body if it is eaten with some oil, so raw tomatoes are ideally accompanied by a vinaigrette or olive-base dressing.

MAJOR NUTRIENTS PER MEDIUM TOMATO

Calories	18
Total fat	0.2 g
Protein	0.9 g
Carbohydrate	3.9 g
Fiber	1.2 g
Vitamin C	12.7 mg
Potassium	237 mg
Lycopene	2,573 mcg
Lutein/Zeaxanthin	123 mcg

Did you know?

Lycopene is actually more active in processed tomato products, such as ketchup, tomato paste, and tomato juice, than it is in the raw tomato.

Tomato sauce

MAKES 2½ CUPS

1 tablespoon olive oil

1 small onion, chopped

2–3 garlic cloves, crushed

1 small celery stalk,
finely chopped

1 bay leaf

4 ripe tomatoes,
peeled and chopped

1 tablespoon tomato paste,
blended with ⅔ cup water

few fresh oregano sprigs

pepper

METHOD

1   Heat the oil in a heavy saucepan over medium heat. Add the onion, garlic, celery, and bay leaf, and cook, stirring frequently, for 5 minutes.

2   Stir in the tomatoes and the tomato paste. Season with pepper and add the oregano. Bring to a boil, then reduce the heat, cover, and simmer, stirring occasionally, for 20–25 minutes, until the tomatoes have completely collapsed. Simmer for an additional 20 minutes to make a thicker sauce, if preferred.

3   Discard the bay leaf and oregano. Transfer to a blender or food processor and process until a chunky puree forms. If a smooth sauce is preferred, pass through a fine nonmetallic strainer. Taste and adjust the seasoning, if necessary. Reheat and use as required.

14

Spinach

Contrary to popular belief, spinach doesn't contain noteworthy levels of iron; nevertheless, it does have many excellent nutritional properties.

Researchers have found that many flavonoid compounds in spinach act as antioxidants and fight against stomach, skin, breast, prostate, and other cancers. Spinach is also extremely high in carotenes, which protect eyesight. It is particularly rich in vitamin K, which helps to boost bone strength and may help prevent osteoporosis. In addition to this, spinach contains peptides, which are aspects of protein that have been shown to lower blood pressure, and its relatively high vitamin E content may help protect the brain from age-related cognitive decline.

- Contains alpha-lipoic acid and glutathione to help retain healthy brain function.
- Source of folate, needed for cell growth, energy, and renewal.
- Contains good levels of essential amino acids, crucial for bone and muscle repair.
- Iron content helps distribute oxygen around the body, which, in turn, is necessary for cell replenishment.

MAJOR NUTRIENTS PER 3½ CUPS/3½ OZ. SPINACH

Calories	23
Total fat	0.4 g
Protein	2.2 g
Carbohydrate	3.6 g
Fiber	2.2 g
Vitamin C	28 mg
Vitamin A	9,377 IU
Beta-carotene	5,626 mcg
Vitamin E	2.03 mg
Vitamin K	483 mg
Folate	194 mg
Calcium	99 mg
Magnesium	79 mg
Iron	2,071 mg

Did you know?

Spinach contains the chemical tyramine, which increases the release of stimulating brain chemicals. If you don't sleep well, avoid these foods close to bedtime.

Practical tips:

Avoid buying spinach with any yellowing leaves; in fact, the darker the leaves, the higher the levels of nutrients contained within. The carotenes in spinach are better absorbed when the leaves are cooked compared to when eaten raw, and also if eaten with a little oil. Steaming or stir-frying retains the most antioxidants. To cook, simply wash the leaves and cook in only the water still clinging to the leaves, stirring if necessary.

Red curry with mixed greens

SERVES 4

2 tablespoons peanut oil or vegetable oil

2 onions, thinly sliced

1 bunch of asparagus spears

1¾ cups reduced-fat coconut milk

2 tablespoons red curry paste

3 fresh kaffir lime leaves

8 cups (about 8 ounces) baby spinach leaves

2 heads bok choy, chopped

1 small head napa cabbage, shredded

handful of fresh cilantro, chopped

cooked rice, to serve

METHOD

1   Heat a wok or skillet over medium–high heat. Add the oil and heat for 30 seconds. Add the onions and asparagus spears and stir-fry for 1–2 minutes.

2   Add the coconut milk, curry paste, and lime leaves and bring gently to a boil. Add the spinach, bok choy, and cabbage and cook for 2–3 minutes, until wilted. Stir in the cilantro and serve with rice.

Garlic

Valued as a health protector for thousands of years, garlic bulbs are a useful antibiotic and are also believed to reduce the risk of both heart disease and cancer.

MAJOR NUTRIENTS PER 2 GARLIC CLOVES

Calories	9
Total fat	Trace
Protein	0.4 g
Carbohydrate	2 g
Fiber	Trace
Vitamin C	2 mg
Potassium	24 mg
Calcium	11 mg
Selenium	11 mg

Although often used in only small quantities, garlic can still have a positive effect on health. It contains powerful sulfur compounds, which cause garlic's characteristic strong odor but are also the main source of its health benefits. Research has found that regularly eating garlic could help minimize the risk of heart disease and many types of cancer. It is a powerful antibiotic and inhibits fungal infections, such as athlete's foot. It also appears to minimize stomach ulcers. Eaten in reasonable quantity, garlic is a good source of vitamin C, selenium, potassium, and calcium.

- May prevent formation of blood clots and arterial plaque and as a result prevent heart disease.
- Regular garlic consumption can reduce the risk of colon, stomach, and prostate cancers.
- Natural antibiotic, antiviral, and antifungal.
- Could help to prevent stomach ulcers.

Did you know?

Cooking meat at high temperatures can have a carcinogenic effect, but when garlic is used with the meat, it reduces the production of the cancer-promoting chemicals.

Practical tips:
Choose large, firm undamaged garlic bulbs and store in a container with air holes in a dark, cool, dry place. Skin the garlic by lightly crushing the clove with the flat side of a knife and only lightly cook—long cooking destroys its beneficial compounds. Crush or chop garlic and let stand for a few minutes prior to cooking. Eating parsley after a garlic meal may reduce any mouth odor.

Garlic mushrooms

SERVES 4

2 garlic bulbs

2 tablespoons olive oil

12 ounces cremini mushrooms, halved if large

1 tablespoon chopped fresh parsley

8 scallions, cut into 1-inch lengths

salt and pepper

METHOD

1   Preheat the oven to 350°F. Separate the garlic bulbs into cloves and lightly crush them. Place in an ovenproof dish. Drizzle 2 teaspoons of the oil over the garlic cloves, season generously with salt and pepper, and roast in the preheated oven for 30 minutes.

2   Remove the garlic from the oven and drizzle with 1 teaspoon of the remaining oil. Return to the oven and roast for an additional 45 minutes. Remove from the oven and let cool, then peel the cloves.

3   Heat a skillet over medium heat. Add the oil from the roasting dish, the remaining oil, and the mushrooms to the skillet and cook, stirring frequently, for 4 minutes.

4   Add the garlic cloves, parsley, and scallions and cook, stirring frequently, for 5 minutes. Season with salt and pepper and serve immediately.

Kale

A very nutritious member of the brassica (cabbage) family, kale has the highest levels of antioxidants of all vegetables and is a good source of vitamin C.

Kale is one of the most nutritious members of the brassica family. It is the vegetable with the highest antioxidant capacity, and also contains more calcium and iron than any other vegetable. A single portion contains twice the recommended daily amount of vitamin C, which helps the vegetable's high iron content to be absorbed by the body when ingested. One 3½-cup (3½-ounce) portion also has about one-fifth of the daily calcium requirement for an adult. Kale is rich in selenium, which helps fight cancer, and it contains magnesium and vitamin E for a healthy heart. There are over 45 different flavonoids in kale that combine antioxidant and anti-inflammatory benefits.

- Rich in flavonoids and antioxidants to fight cancers.
- Contains indoles, which can help lower bad cholesterol and prevent cancer.
- Calcium-rich for healthy bones.
- Extremely rich in carotenes to protect eyes.

MAJOR NUTRIENTS PER 1½ CUPS / 3½ OZ. CHOPPED KALE

Calories	50
Total fat	0.7 g
Protein	3.3 g
Carbohydrate	10 g
Fiber	2 g
Vitamin C	120 mg
Folate	29 mcg
Vitamin E	1.7 mg
Potassium	447 mg
Magnesium	34 mg
Calcium	135 mg
Iron	1.7 mg
Selenium	0.9 mcg
Beta-carotene	9,226 mcg
Lutein/Zeaxanthin	39,550 mcg

Did you know?

Kale contains naturally occurring substances that can interfere with the functioning of the thyroid glands—people with thryoid problems may not want to eat kale.

Practical tips:

Always wash kale before use because the curly leaves may contain grit or soil. Don't discard the outer, deep green leaves—these contain high amounts of beneficial carotenes and indoles. Treat kale as you would cabbage—it is good steamed or stir-fried. It has a strong taste that goes well with bacon, eggs, and cheese. Kale, like spinach, shrinks a lot during cooking, so make sure you add plenty to the pan.

Kale stir-fry

SERVES 4

1½ pounds fresh kale

2 tablespoons sunflower oil

1 onion, chopped

4 large garlic cloves, finely chopped

2 red bell peppers, thinly sliced

1 carrot, peeled and shredded

1½ cups broccoli florets

pinch of crushed red pepper (optional)

½ cup vegetable stock

1 cup fresh bean sprouts

salt and pepper

handful of chopped, toasted cashew nuts, to garnish

lemon wedges, to serve

METHOD

1 Using a sharp knife, remove any thick cores in the middle of the kale leaves and slice finely. Set aside.

2 Heat a wok or skillet over high heat. Add the oil and heat for 30 seconds. Add the onion and stir-fry for about 3 minutes, then add the garlic, bell peppers, and carrot and stir-fry until the onion is tender and the peppers are starting to soften. Add the broccoli and crushed red pepper, if using, and stir.

3 Add the kale to the wok and stir, then add the stock and season with salt and pepper. Reduce the heat to medium and simmer for about 5 minutes, until the kale is tender.

4 Use two forks to mix the bean sprouts through the other ingredients in the wok, then adjust the seasoning, if necessary. Serve the vegetables sprinkled with the cashew nuts.

Celery

Typically seen as a dieting snack, celery is high in potassium and calcium and helps to reduce fluid retention and prevent high blood pressure.

Celery has long been regarded as an ideal food for dieters because of its high water content and resulting low calorie content. In fact, celery is a useful and healthy vegetable for many other reasons—it is also a good source of potassium and is surprisingly high in calcium, which is vital for healthy bones, healthy blood pressure levels, and nerve function. The darker green stalks and the leaves of celery contain higher levels of vitamins and minerals than the paler leaves, so don't discard them. Celery also contains the compounds polyacetylenes and phthalides, which may protect us from inflammation and high blood pressure.

- Low in calories and fat and high in fiber.
- Good source of potassium.
- Calcium content protects bones and may help regulate blood pressure.
- May offer protection from inflammation.

Practical tips:
Choose celery heads with leaves that look bright green and fresh. Store in a plastic bag or in plastic wrap to prevent the stalks turning limp. Celery is ideal for adding flavor and bulk to soups and stews and the stalks can be braised in vegetable stock for an excellent accompaniment to fish, poultry, or game. The leaves can be added to salads and stir-fries or used as a garnish.

MAJOR NUTRIENTS PER 2½ STALKS/3½ OZ. CELERY

Calories	16
Total fat	0.17 g
Protein	0.69 g
Carbohydrate	2.97 g
Fiber	1.6 g
Vitamin C	3.1 mg
Vitamin B_3	0.32 mg
Vitamin B_5	0.25 mg
Folate	36 mg
Calcium	40 mg
Magnesium	11 mg
Potassium	260 mg

Celery & apple revitalizer

SERVES 2

3 celery stalks, chopped

1 Red Delicious or other crisp apple, peeled, cored, and diced

2½ cups low-fat milk

pinch of sugar (optional)

salt (optional)

strips of celery, for decorating

METHOD

1 Place the celery, apple, and milk in a blender and process until thoroughly combined.

2 Stir in the sugar and some salt, if using. Pour into chilled glasses, decorate with strips of celery, and serve.

18

Peas

Whether freshly picked or bought frozen, peas are packed with vitamin C, are a rich source of fiber, and also contain lutein, which is important for healthy eyes.

Peas are rich in a wide range of useful vitamins and minerals. They are particularly high in antioxidants, such as vitamin C, folate, and vitamin B_3, and their very high lutein and zeaxanthin content means that they help protect the eyes from macular degeneration. The B vitamins they contain may help protect the bones from osteoporosis, and they may help to decrease the risk of strokes by keeping levels of the amino acid homocysteine low in the blood. Peas are also an important source of protein for those on restricted diets, such as vegetarians. In addition, their high fiber content partly comprises pectin, a jellylike substance that helps to lower bad blood cholesterol and may also help prevent heart and arterial disease.

- Contain several heart-friendly nutrients and chemicals.
- Rich in carotenes to protect eyes and reduce risk of cancers.
- High in total and soluble fiber, which could lower cholesterol.
- Very rich in vitamin C.

Practical tips:
When buying peas in the pod, choose those that aren't packed in too tightly. Older peas become almost square, lose their flavor, and become mealy because the sugars have been converted to starches. Young pods can be eaten with the peas inside and young peas can be eaten raw. To cook, steam lightly or boil in minimal water, because the vitamin C content diminishes in water.

MAJOR NUTRIENTS PER ⅔ CUP/3½ OZ. SHELLED PEAS

Calories	81
Total fat	0.4 g
Protein	5.4 g
Carbohydrate	14.5 g
Fiber	5.1 g
Vitamin C	40 mg
Vitamin E	Trace
Folate	65 mcg
Potassium	244 mg
Lutein/Zeaxanthin	2,477 mcg

Did you know?

Frozen peas can often contain more vitamin C and other nutrients than fresh peas in their pods, which may be several days old.

Chilled pea soup

SERVES 4

2 cups vegetable stock or water
3 cups frozen peas
3 scallions, coarsely chopped
1¼ cups plain yogurt
salt and pepper

TO GARNISH
2 tablespoons chopped fresh mint
grated lemon rind
olive oil

METHOD

1 Bring the stock to a boil in a large saucepan over medium heat. Reduce the heat, add the peas and scallions, and simmer for 5 minutes.

2 Let cool slightly, then blend until smooth using a handheld immersion blender or a food processor. Pour into a large bowl, season with salt and pepper, and stir in the yogurt. Cover the bowl with plastic wrap and chill in the refrigerator for several hours, or until well chilled.

3 To serve, remove from the refrigerator, mix well, and ladle into soup bowls. Garnish with the chopped mint, grated lemon rind, and a drizzle of olive oil.

19

Beets

These colorful, sweet roots may not be the richest vegetable in nutrients, but they certainly should not be overlooked and are invaluable during the winter season.

Beets come in white and gold varieties as well as the classic purple-red, which is the best source of nutrients. Betaine, which gives them their deep color, is even more potent an antioxidant than polyphenols in its effect on lowering blood pressure. A scientific study also found that the high levels of nitrates in beet juice work like aspirin to prevent blood clots, and help to protect the lining of the blood vessels. Red beets are also rich in anthocyanins, which may help to prevent colon and other cancers.

- Betaine helps lower blood pressure and has anti-inflammatory properties.
- Contain nitrates, which help prevent blood clots.
- Anthocyanins can help prevent cancers.
- A good source of iron, magnesium, and folate.

Practical tips:
Cooked beets will keep in an airtight container in the refrigerator for a few days, or you can puree cooked beets and freeze them. To cook, cut off the leaves so that about 2 inches of stems remain, and keep the root in place. This will prevent the beets from "bleeding" as they cook. Beets can be boiled whole for about 50 minutes or brushed with a little oil and baked in aluminum foil at 400°F for 1 hour. The skins can then be easily rubbed off. Beets can also be used raw, peeled and shredded into salads or salsa, or juiced.

MAJOR NUTRIENTS PER 1¼ CUPS/3½ OZ. BEETS

Calories	36
Total fat	Trace
Protein	1.7 g
Carbohydrate	7.6 g
Fiber	1.9 g
Vitamin C	5 mg
Folate	150 mg
Potassium	380 mg
Calcium	20 mg
Iron	1.0 mg
Magnesium	23 mg

Beet & spinach salad

SERVES 4

3 tablespoons extra virgin
olive oil

juice of 1 orange

1 teaspoon sugar

1 teaspoon fennel seeds

5 cups diced, cooked beets

1 (4-ounce) package fresh
baby spinach leaves

salt and pepper

METHOD

1   Heat the olive oil in a small, heavy saucepan. Add the orange
juice, sugar, and fennel seeds and season with salt and pepper.
Stir continuously until the sugar has dissolved.

2   Add the beets to the saucepan and stir gently to coat. Remove
from the heat.

3   Arrange the spinach leaves in a large salad bowl. Spoon
the warm beets on top and serve immediately.

Leeks

Members of the health-giving allium family, along with garlic and onions, leeks contain a combination of nutrients for healthy skin, bones, and heart.

MAJOR NUTRIENTS PER AVERAGE LEEK

Calories	61
Total fat	0.3 g
Protein	1.5 g
Carbohydrate	2.9 g
Fiber	1.8 g
Vitamin C	12 mg
Vitamin B$_6$	0.23 mg
Vitamin K	47 mcg
Folate	64 mcg
Calcium	59 mcg
Magnesium	28 mg

Leeks have a distinct, slightly sweet, onion flavor but are milder than most onions. The long, thick stems have a lower white area and dark green tops, which are edible but are usually removed because they can be tough. Leeks have been shown to reduce total bad blood cholesterol while raising good cholesterol, and so can help to prevent heart and arterial disease. Regular consumption is also linked with a reduction in the risk of prostate, ovarian, and colon cancers. It is the allylic sulfides in the plants that appear to confer these cancer-fighting benefits, but they are also rich in vitamin C, fiber, vitamin E, folate, and several important minerals.

• Lower total bad cholesterol levels in the blood and raise good cholesterol.
• Mildly diuretic to help prevent fluid retention.
• High in carotenes, including lutein and zeaxanthin, for eye health.

Practical tips:
Wash leeks thoroughly before using—they may contain soil between the tight leaves. The more of the green section of the leek that you use, the more of the beneficial nutrients you will retain. Instead of boiling, steam, bake, or stir-fry leeks to retain their vitamins. The darker green parts take a little longer to cook than the white part, so, if chopped, add the green parts to the pan first.

Leek & chicken soup

SERVES 6-8

2 tablespoons olive oil
2 onions, coarsely chopped
2 carrots, peeled and chopped
5 leeks, 2 coarsely chopped, 3 thinly sliced
3-pound chicken, skin and fat removed
2 bay leaves
6 prunes, sliced
salt and pepper
fresh parsley sprigs, to garnish

METHOD

1 Heat the oil in a large saucepan over medium heat. Add the onions, carrots, and the coarsely chopped leeks and sauté for 3–4 minutes, until just golden brown.

2 Place the chicken in the saucepan with the cooked vegetables and add the bay leaves. Pour in enough cold water to cover and season well with salt and pepper. Bring to a boil, reduce the heat, then cover and simmer for 1–1½ hours, skimming off any foam that rises to the surface with a slotted spoon. Cook until the chicken is tender and the juices run clear when the tip of a sharp knife is inserted into the thickest part of the meat.

3 Remove the chicken from the stock, then remove all the meat and cut into bite-size pieces. Strain the stock through a colander, discarding the vegetables and bay leaves, and return to the rinsed-out saucepan. Skim any fat from the surface.

4 Heat the stock to simmering point. Add the sliced leeks and prunes and heat for about 1 minute.

5 Return the cooked chicken to the pan and heat through. Ladle the soup into warm soup bowls and serve garnished with parsley sprigs.

21

Pumpkin

Pumpkins contain the orange nutrients alpha- and beta-carotene and lutein, powerful antiaging nutrients that protect your skin against damage from sunlight.

The fat-soluble carotenoids contained in pumpkin are needed to protect fatty areas in the skin, heart, eyes, brain, and liver. As a winter vegetable, pumpkin is well placed to protect the body when it is most needed—we eat more fat in the winter and lay down more fat stores for insulation. The seeds of the pumpkin are incredibly nutrient-rich, while the orange flesh contains malic acid—also found in apples and plums—that is needed by every cell in the body for renewal. In combination with the protective carotenoids, malic acid helps to keep skin firm, bones strong, and vital organs healthy.

- Contains phytosterols, needed for immune function and cholesterol regulation.
- Contains vitamin B_2 to activate folate, and vitamin B_6 to process fats and proteins from food to repair and rejuvenate body tissues and mucous membranes.

MAJOR NUTRIENTS PER 1 CUP/3½ OZ. PUMPKIN

Calories	13
Total fat	0.1 g
Protein	1 g
Carbohydrate	6.5 g
Fiber	0.5 g
Vitamin C	9 mg
Vitamin E	1.06 mg
Vitamin B_2	0.11 mg
Vitamin B_6	0.06 mg
Folate	16 mcg
Beta-carotene	3,100 mcg
Lutein/Zeaxanthin	1,500 mcg
Phytosterols	12 mg

Did you know?

The name "pumpkin" originally comes from the Greek *peponi*, meaning "large melon." The French called it *pompon*, and the British opted for *pumpion*, before the American name came about.

Practical tips:

Like most squash, pumpkin can be boiled, steamed, baked, or roasted, and it can be used to make both sweet desserts and unsweetened dishes. Pumpkin is sometimes oversweetened, which masks its delicate flavor. Try roasting your own pumpkin seeds in the oven for a healthy snack.

Carrot & pumpkin curry

SERVES 4

⅔ cup vegetable stock

1-inch piece fresh galangal, sliced

2 garlic cloves, chopped

1 lemongrass stalk (white part only), finely chopped

2 fresh red chiles, seeded and chopped

4 carrots, peeled and cut into chunks

2 cups peeled, seeded, and diced pumpkin

2 tablespoons peanut oil

2 shallots, finely chopped

3 tablespoons Thai yellow curry paste

1¾ cups canned coconut milk

4–6 fresh Thai basil sprigs

2 tablespoons lightly toasted pumpkin seeds, to garnish

METHOD

1   Pour the stock into a large saucepan and bring to a boil. Add the galangal, half the garlic, the lemongrass, and chiles and simmer for 5 minutes. Add the carrots and pumpkin and simmer for an additional 5–6 minutes, until tender.

2   Meanwhile, heat a wok over high heat. Add the oil and heat for 30 seconds. Add the shallots and the remaining garlic and stir-fry for 2–3 minutes. Add the curry paste and stir-fry for an additional 1–2 minutes.

3   Add the shallot mixture to the saucepan along with the coconut milk and Thai basil. Simmer for 2–3 minutes. Serve hot, sprinkled with the toasted pumpkin seeds.

22

Turkey

A low-fat, high protein source, turkey is a versatile alternative to chicken—quick and easy to prepare, it's easy to incorporate into the modern diet.

Turkey is known for its high tryptophan content, which is a protein constituent from which the body makes the mood, sleep, and appetite-regulating brain chemical serotonin. Turkey's high protein content also helps control appetite by balancing blood sugar concentration, so curbing sugar cravings and energy fluctuations. The white meat of turkey is considered healthier than the brown meat due to its lower fat content, but the difference is small. In fact, the brown meat can actually help raise your metabolism more, making you more efficient at burning fuel, more likely to lose weight, and less susceptible to overeating.

- Iron supports energy levels by producing the cells that your body uses for fuel and helping muscles store rejuvenating oxygen.
- Glutamic acid helps balance blood sugar levels.
- Contains the zinc that is needed to make serotonin, which makes you feel good. It is also vital in the process of repair to the body.

Practical tips:
Turkey can be a lower fat alternative to chicken, with many similar health benefits. A pasture-raised bird that has had a healthy diet itself and lived more naturally will be leaner, taste better, and lose less water when cooked. Prepare and cook in the same way as you would chicken.

MAJOR NUTRIENTS PER 3½ OZ. TURKEY, SKIN REMOVED

Calories	111
Total fat	0.65 g
Saturated fat	0.21 g
Monounsaturated fat	0.11 g
Protein	24.6 g
Carbohydrate	0 mg
Fiber	0 mg
Vitamin B_3	6.23 mg
Vitamin B_5	0.72 mg
Vitamin B_6	0.58 mg
Iron	1.17 mg
Zinc	1.24 mg
Glutamic acid	4.02 g

Turkey salad pita bread

MAKES 1

small handful of baby spinach, rinsed, patted dry and shredded

½ red bell pepper, seeded and thinly sliced

½ carrot, peeled and shredded

¼ cup hummus

⅔ cup thinly sliced, cooked boneless, skinless turkey

½ tablespoon sunflower seeds

1 whole-wheat pita bread

salt and pepper

METHOD

1 Preheat the broiler to high.

2 Put the spinach, red bell pepper, carrot, and hummus into a large bowl and stir together, so all the salad ingredients are coated with the hummus. Stir in the turkey and sunflower seeds and season with salt and pepper.

3 Put the pita bread under the broiler for about 1 minute on each side to warm through, but do not brown. Cut it in half to make two "pockets" of bread.

4 Divide the salad between the bread pockets and serve.

Chicken

A single serving of protein-rich, pasture-raised chicken provides two-thirds of the nutrients needed by the body to replenish skin, bone, and muscle.

MAJOR NUTRIENTS PER 3½ OZ. CHICKEN, SKIN REMOVED

Calories	114
Total fat	2.59 g
Protein	0 mg
Carbohydrate	0 mg
Fiber	10.43 mg
Vitamin C	0 mg
Potassium	Trace
Lycopene	Trace
Lutein/Zeaxanthin	Trace

The human body consists of 22 percent protein, and just under half of this is muscle. Your muscles need continual replenishment, especially after exercise, in order for the body to maintain mobility and posture. Stress uses up protein in the body to make adrenaline, but protein-rich foods, such as chicken, in the diet can replace it in a way that the body finds easy to absorb. Chicken that has been reared in a healthy, pasture-raised environment can also provide the B vitamins needed to maintain energy levels and good brain function.

- Protein makes collagen, which is needed on a daily basis to rejuvenate skin, hair, nails, and the internal organs.
- Contains hyaluronic acid, which holds water in collagen in order to keep the body hydrated.
- Contains glutamic acid, the main protein in human muscle, which provides strength and rapid regeneration.
- The antioxidant mineral selenium helps combat toxic metals, such as mercury, lead, and aluminum.

Practical tips:
Choose your chicken wisely—birds raised in confined spaces will not have used their muscles enough to develop as a source of protein and can also be much higher in fat than pasture-raised birds. Although it is a more expensive option, organic chicken is a better quality and worth the extra cost.

Thai-spiced chicken

SERVES 4

1 tablespoon olive oil
1 garlic clove, finely chopped
1-inch piece fresh ginger, peeled and finely chopped
1 small fresh red chile, seeded and finely chopped
12 ounces skinless, boneless pasture-raised chicken breasts, cut into thin strips
1 tablespoon Thai seven-spice seasoning
1 red bell pepper and 1 yellow pepper, seeded and sliced
2 zucchini, thinly sliced
1 (8-ounce) can bamboo shoots, drained
2 tablespoons apple juice
1 tablespoon light soy sauce
2 tablespoons chopped fresh cilantro, plus extra to garnish
salt and pepper

METHOD

1 Heat a wok or skillet over high heat. Add the oil and heat for 30 seconds. Add the garlic, ginger, and chile and stir-fry for 30 seconds to release the flavors.

2 Add the chicken and Thai seasoning and stir-fry for about 4 minutes, or until the chicken has browned all over. Add the bell peppers and zucchini and stir-fry for 1–2 minutes, or until slightly softened.

3 Stir in the bamboo shoots and stir-fry for another 2–3 minutes, or until the chicken is cooked through and tender. Add the apple juice, soy sauce, and seasoning and let sizzle for 1–2 minutes.

4 Stir in the chopped cilantro and serve immediately, garnished with extra cilantro.

24

Grass-fed beef

Grass-fed beef raised on pasture grazing provides essential fats often lacking in the diet, which can help to keep the skin, bones, and heart healthy.

Grass-fed cattle generally get more exercise, making their meat leaner, and for every 3-ounce serving, there is around ¼ ounce less fat in grass-fed beef than in its grain-fed counterpart. This is good news for calorie counters, but, more importantly, the quality of fat contained in grass-fed beef is better. Grass-fed beef contains high levels of omega-3 oils, which keep the heart, joints, brain, and skin youthful. Another fat, CLA (conjugated linoleic acid), comes direct from the grass, and enables stored fat to be burned as energy, raising the metabolism and helping maintain a trim figure. Low levels of CLA in our diet have been partly linked to the rise of obesity.

- Contains four times more vitamin E than grain-fed beef.
- Good selenium levels lessen anxiety, depression, and fatigue—low levels are associated with heart and bone degeneration.
- Contains the highest level of zinc in any meat, promoting clear skin and strong nails.
- Coenzyme Q-10 increases energy in all cells, especially the heart.

Practical tips:
Ask your butcher for the best source or find a farm shop attached to its own pasture. Top sirloin, tenderloin, and flank steak are the healthiest, leanest cuts. This is a nutrient dense food, so you need to eat it only 2–4 times a month to get the benefits.

MAJOR NUTRIENTS PER 3½ OZ. BEEF, GRASS-FED

Calories	192
Total fat	12.73 g
Saturated fat	5.34 g
Protein	19.42 g
Fiber	0 mg
Vitamin B$_3$	4.82 mg
Vitamin B$_5$	0.58 mg
Vitamin B$_6$	0.36 mg
Vitamin B$_{12}$	1.97 mg
Viitamin E	930 mcg
Iron	1.99 mg
Zinc	4.55 mg
Selenium	14.2 mcg

Spicy beef stir-fry

SERVES 4

1 teaspoon olive oil

5 ounces grass-fed, pasture-raised top sirloin steak (fat removed), cut into thin strips

1 orange bell pepper, seeded and cut into thin strips

4 scallions, trimmed and chopped

1–2 fresh jalapeño chiles, seeded and chopped

2–3 garlic cloves, chopped

1½ cups trimmed and diagonally halved snow peas, trimmed and cut in half diagonally

4 ounces large portobello mushrooms, sliced

1 teaspoon hoisin sauce, or to taste

1 tablespoon fresh orange juice

5 cups arugula or watercress

METHOD

1 Heat a large wok or skillet over high heat. Add the oil and heat for 30 seconds. Add the beef and stir-fry for 1 minute, or until browned. Using a slotted spoon, remove and reserve.

2 Add the bell pepper, scallions, chiles, and garlic and stir-fry for 2 minutes. Add the snow peas and mushrooms and stir-fry for an additional 2 minutes.

3 Return the beef to the wok and add the hoisin sauce and orange juice. Stir-fry for 2–3 minutes, or until the beef is tender and the vegetables are tender but still firm to the bite. Stir in the arugula and stir-fry until it starts to wilt. Serve immediately, divided equally among four warm bowls.

25

Venison

Venison has recently grown in popularity. It is similar to beef but is leaner, providing dense protein without the heart-clogging saturated fat content.

MAJOR NUTRIENTS PER 3½ OZ. VENISON

Calories	157
Total fat	7.13 g
Saturated fat	3.36 g
Protein	21.78 g
Carbohydrate	0 mg
Fiber	0 mg
Vitamin B_2	0.55 mg
Vitamin B_3	0.69 mg
Vitamin B_5	0.75 mg
Vitamin B_6	32 mcg
Vitamin B_{12}	3.15 g
Iron	2.92 g
Zinc	4.2 mg
Selenium	10 mg

This protein combines with a great B vitamin profile to keep the body intact and youthful. It includes the sulfur amino acids taurine and cystine, which are key in aiding the liver to rid the body of toxins as part of the metabolic process. If these are allowed to keep circulating, the body becomes tired, ill, and unable to heal and renew. Taurine and cystine also help hold essential minerals in the body, tonify the blood, prevent heart disease, and improve circulation to keep skin healthy and glowing.

- Vitamins B_{12} and B_6 clear the brain and heart of the substance homocysteine, which can lead to dementia and heart disease.
- Vitamin B_3 keeps joints mobile and prevents osteoarthritis.
- Contains zinc, which revitalizes the skin and keeps pores clear.
- Zinc and selenium in combination create detoxification enzymes that rejuvenate cells all over the body.
- Iron moves oxygen around the body for efficient healing.

Practical tips:
Ask your butcher to let you know when venison is in season. If you buy at this time, from animals that have been hunted, you'll benefit from an absence of aging additives. Venison should be frozen for a minimum of two hours before use to kill off any parasites or tapeworms. Broil venison steaks and cook less tender cuts in a hearty winter stew with root vegetables and spices.

Charbroiled venison steaks

SERVES 4

4 venison steaks
fresh thyme sprigs, to garnish

MARINADE
⅔ cup red wine
2 tablespoons olive oil
1 tablespoon red wine vinegar
1 onion, chopped
1 tablespoon chopped fresh parsley
1 tablespoon chopped fresh thyme
1 bay leaf
1 teaspoon good-quality honey
½ teaspoon mild mustard
salt and pepper

METHOD

1 Place the venison steaks in a shallow, nonmetallic dish.

2 To make the marinade, add the wine, oil, wine vinegar, onion, fresh parsley, thyme, bay leaf, honey, and mustard to a bowl, season with salt and pepper, and beat vigorously, until well combined.

3 Pour the marinade over the venison, cover, and let marinate in the refrigerator overnight. Turn the steaks occasionally so that the meat is well coated.

4 Preheat the broiler to high. Cook the venison under the hot broiler for 2 minutes on each side to seal the meat.

5 Turn down the broiler to medium, and cook for an additional 4–10 minutes on each side, according to taste. Test by inserting the tip of a knife into the meat—the juices will range from red when the meat is still rare to clear as the meat becomes well cooked.

6 Transfer the steaks to serving plates, garnish with fresh thyme sprigs, and serve.

Salmon

Salmon is an excellent source of omega-3 fats, cancer-fighting selenium, and vitamin B$_{12}$, which helps protect against heart disease and a form of anemia.

The salmon that we eat today is often farmed instead of wild. Although wild salmon tends to contain less fat and slightly higher levels of some nutrients, the two kinds are broadly comparable. Salmon is an important source of fish oils, which provide protection against heart disease, blood clots, strokes, high blood pressure, high blood cholesterol, Alzheimer's disease, depression, and certain skin conditions. Salmon is also an excellent source of selenium, which protects against cancer, plus protein, niacin, vitamin B$_{12}$, magnesium, and vitamin B$_6$.

- Protection against cardiovascular diseases and strokes.
- Helps keep the brain healthy and improve insulin resistance.
- Contains good levels of docosahexaenoic (DHA) and eicosapentaenoic (EPA)—vital for maintaining brain and eye health.
- Helps minimize joint pain and may protect against cancers.

Practical tips:
Where possible, buy wild salmon—although just as high in nutrients, farmed salmon has been found to contain up to twice the amount of fat. For optimum omega-3 content, instead of pan-frying, cook salmon lightly and poach or broil. Overcooking can oxidize the essential fats, and this means that they are no longer beneficial. Frozen salmon retains the beneficial oils, vitamins, and minerals, while canned salmon loses a proportion of these nutrients.

MAJOR NUTRIENTS PER 3½ OZ. SALMON

Calories	183
Total fat	10.8 g
Protein	19.9 g
EPA	0.618 g
DHA	1.293 g
Niacin	7.5 mg
Vitamin B$_6$	0.64 mcg
Vitamin B$_{12}$	2.8 mcg
Folate	26 mcg
Vitamin E	1.9 mg
Vitamin C	3.9 mg
Potassium	362 mg
Selenium	36.5 mcg
Magnesium	28 mg
Zinc	0.4 mg

Salmon & scallop stir-fry

SERVES 6

⅓ cup peanut oil

12 ounces salmon fillet, skinned and cut into 1-inch chunks

8 ounces fresh scallops, shelled

3 carrots, thinly sliced

2 celery stalks, cut into 1-inch pieces

2 yellow bell peppers, thinly sliced

6 ounces oyster mushrooms, thinly sliced

1 garlic clove, crushed

⅓ cup chopped fresh cilantro

3 shallots, thinly sliced

juice of 2 limes

1 teaspoon lime zest

1 teaspoon crushed red pepper

3 tablespoons dry sherry

3 tablespoons soy sauce

cooked noodles, to serve

METHOD

1   Heat a large wok or skillet over medium heat. Add the oil and heat for 30 seconds. Add the salmon and scallops and stir-fry for 3 minutes. Remove from the wok and keep warm.

2   Add the carrots, celery, bell peppers, mushrooms, and garlic to the wok and stir-fry for 3 minutes. Stir in the cilantro and shallots.

3   Stir in the lime juice and zest, crushed red pepper, sherry, and soy sauce, then return the salmon and scallops to the wok and stir-fry for an additional 1–2 minutes, until warmed through. Transfer to warmed individual serving plates and serve immediately on a bed of cooked noodles.

27

Tuna

Fresh tuna is an important source of omega-3 fats and antioxidant minerals for arterial and heart health, and it is also rich in vitamin E for healthy skin.

The firm, meaty flesh of fresh or frozen tuna is an ideal choice of fish for nonfish lovers and is also simple to prepare and quick to cook. It is an excellent source of protein and is especially rich in the B vitamins, selenium, and magnesium. A small portion will contain around 20 percent of your daily vitamin E needs. While most types of tuna contain fewer of the essential omega-3 fats than some other oily fishes do, there is still a good content of benefitical fats. DHA fats are particularly effective in keeping our hearts and brains healthy and in good working order. Just one portion of tuna a week can provide the recommended 1.4 g of these fats a week.

- A good source of omega-3, EPA, and DHA fats, which offer protection against a range of diseases.
- Rich in selenium and magnesium for heart health.
- Extremely rich in vitamin B_{12} for healthy blood.

Practical tips:
Fresh fish should be odorless, with bright, clear eyes, and it is best cooked and eaten on the day of purchase. To retain all the health benefits of the omega-3 fats, lightly sear tuna in a skillet on both sides and cook for as little time as you can. Tuna steaks can also be sliced and stir-fried with vegetables—unlike many types of fish, it has a meaty texture and the slices won't disintegrate when cooked.

MAJOR NUTRIENTS PER 3½ OZ. TUNA

Calories	144
Total fat	4.9 g
Protein	23 g
EPA	0.4 g
DHA	1.2 g
Niacin	8.3 mg
Vitamin B_5	1 mg
Vitamin B_6	0.5 mg
Vitamin B_{12}	9.4 mg
Vitamin E	1 mg
Potassium	252 mg
Selenium	36 mcg
Magnesium	50 mg
Iron	1 mg
Zinc	0.6 mg

Did you know?

Research has found that when tuna is canned it loses most of its beneficial omega-3 fats, so it shouldn't count toward your oily fish intake.

Seared tuna & bean salad

SERVES 6   METHOD

½ cup extra virgin olive oil, plus extra for brushing

juice of 1 lemon

½ teaspoon crushed red pepper

¼ teaspoon coarsely ground black pepper

4 thin fresh tuna steaks, about 4 ounces each

1 (29-ounce) can cannellini beans, well drained and rinsed

1 shallot, finely chopped

1 garlic clove, crushed

2 teaspoons finely chopped fresh rosemary

2 tablespoons chopped fresh flat-leaf parsley

4 artichokes in oil, drained and quartered

4 vine-ripened tomatoes, sliced lengthwise into segments

16 ripe black olives, pitted

salt and pepper

lemon wedges, to serve

1. Place ¼ cup of the oil in a shallow dish with 3 tablespoons of the lemon juice, the crushed red pepper, and black pepper. Add the tuna steaks and let marinate at room temperature for 1 hour, turning occasionally.

2. Add the cannellini beans to a microwavable bowl and heat on medium for 2 minutes. While still warm, toss with the remaining oil, then stir in the shallot, garlic, herbs, and remaining lemon juice. Season with a little salt and plenty of pepper. Let stand for at least 30 minutes.

3. Brush a ridged grill pan or skillet with a little of the oil and place over high heat. Add the tuna to the pan and sear for 1–2 minutes on each side. Transfer the steaks to a cutting board, reduce the heat to low, and add the marinade to the pan to cook for 1–2 minutes.

4. Transfer the beans to a serving dish. Mix together the beans, artichokes, tomatoes, and olives and arrange on serving plates. Flake the tuna on top and serve immediately with lemon wedges for squeezing over the salad.

28

Trout

Trout is one of a number of oily fish sources that provide a valuable package of nutrients that safeguard the joints, eyes, and brain from damage.

Omega-3 oils are crucial to mood and behavior regulation because they affect how we use the stabilizing brain chemicals serotonin and dopamine. Eating oily fish one to three times a week has also been shown to improve brain function and slow down the loss in concentration, memory, and mental acuity associated with aging and stress. Of all the oily fish, trout is one of the least contaminated by mercury toxicity. Mercury is common in larger oily fish, such as tuna and swordfish, and, therefore, it should be avoided by young children and pregnant women.

- Contains pink astaxanthin, which supports good eye health and brain development.
- Contains Vitamin D—low levels of which have been linked to occurrences of both depression and dementia.
- High levels of the B vitamins promote increased energy levels.
- Omega-3 oils lubricate joints to ensure pain-free agility.

Practical tips:
Trout can be bought both fresh and smoked. The fresh fish are easy to stuff with herbs and lemon and bake, and the smoked type makes a good alternative to the stronger-flavored salmon. This is an excellent choice of oily fish for people who dislike a strong fishy flavor.

MAJOR NUTRIENTS PER 3½ OZ. SMOKED TROUT

Calories	148
Total fat	6.61 g
EPA	0.2 g
DHA	0.53 g
Protein	20.77 g
Carbohydrate	0 mg
Fiber	0 mg
Vitamin B_1	0.35 mg
Vitamin B_3	4.5 mg
Vitamin B_{12}	7.79 mg
Vitamin D	155 IU

Smoked trout salad

SERVES 4

1 red bell pepper,
halved and seeded

4 smoked trout fillets,
about 5 ounces each,
skinned and flaked

4 scallions, trimmed and chopped

2 large endive heads, halved,
cored, and shredded

1½ tablespoons Chinese rice
wine vinegar

½ tablespoon sunflower oil

2 tablespoons chopped
fresh parsley

radicchio leaves,
rinsed and dried

salt and pepper

METHOD

1 Run a swivel-bladed vegetable peeler along the length of the cut edges of the bell pepper to make very thin slices. Chop the slices and put them in a bowl.

2 Add the trout, scallions, and endive, tossing to mix together. Add 1 tablespoon of the vinegar, the oil, parsley, and salt and pepper and toss again, then add extra vinegar as required.

3 Cover and chill until ready to serve. Arrange the radicchio leaves on individual plates. Toss the salad again and adjust the seasoning, if necessary. Place a portion of salad on each plate of radicchio leaves and serve.

29

Scallops

They may be a luxurious treat but scallops can also help boost your vitamin B$_{12}$ and magnesium intake, which, in turn, could help to protect the arteries and bones.

MAJOR NUTRIENTS PER 3½ OZ. SHELLED SCALLOPS

Calories	88
Total fat	0.8 g
Protein	16.8 g
Vitamin B$_{12}$	1.5 g
Folate	16 mcg
Potassium	314 mg
Selenium	22 mcg
Magnesium	56 mg
Zinc	0.95 mg
Calcium	24 mg

Did you know?

Scallops are rich in tryptophan, an amino acid that helps the production of the mood-enhancing serotonin in our brains and may help cure insomnia.

Scallops are an excellent source of vitamin B$_{12}$, which is needed by the body to deactivate homocysteine, a chemical that can damage blood vessel walls. High homocysteine levels are also linked to osteoporosis. A recent study found that osteoporosis occurred more frequently among women whose vitamin B$_{12}$ was deficient. B$_{12}$ is particularly important for individuals who don't consume red meat as a regular part of their diet. Scallops are also a good source of magnesium and a regular intake helps build bone density, regulate nerves, and keep the heart healthy.

• Low in calories and fat so ideal for dieters.
• Rich in magnesium, which is essential to all cells—magnesium deficiency has been linked to illnesses, such as asthma, diabetes, and osteoporosis.
• A good source of vitamin B$_{12}$ for arterial and bone health.
• Regular intake may help protect against colon cancer.

Practical tips:
Fresh scallops should have flesh that is white and firm, have no evidence of browning, and be free of odor. The orange-pink coral can be either removed or cooked along with the rest of the scallop. Scallops should be cooked for only a few minutes, because exposure to too much heat will cause them to become tough. The sweet flavor of scallops goes well with chile, cilantro, garlic, and parsley.

Scallops on noodles

SERVES 4

4 ounces dried
rice noodles
2 tablespoons butter
1 garlic clove, crushed
pinch of paprika
1 tablespoon peanut oil or
sunflower oil,
plus extra for brushing
2 tablespoons Thai green
curry paste
2 tablespoons water
2 teaspoons light soy sauce
2 scallions, finely shredded,
plus extra, sliced, to
garnish
12 fresh scallops, shelled
salt and pepper

METHOD

1   Cook the noodles in a large saucepan of boiling water
    according to the package directions, then rinse under cold
    running water and drain well.

2   Meanwhile, melt the butter in a small saucepan over low heat.
    Add the garlic and cook, stirring, for 1 minute. Stir in the
    paprika and set aside.

3   Heat a wok or skillet over high heat. Add the oil and heat for
    30 seconds. Add the curry paste, water, and soy sauce and bring
    to a boil. Add the cooked noodles and reheat, stirring gently. Stir
    in the scallions, then remove from the heat and keep warm.

4   Heat a ridged grill pan or skillet over high heat and brush
    lightly with oil. Add the scallops to the pan and cook, brushing
    with the garlic butter, for 3 minutes, then turn over and cook for
    2 minutes on the other side; if cut open, the center shouldn't be
    totally opaque—they continue to cook off the heat. Season with
    salt and pepper. Divide the noodles among four dishes and top
    with three scallops each. Garnish with scallion slices and serve.

30

Oysters

Rich in zinc, oysters are prized for their nutritional qualities, which are thought to boost the immune system and aid the body's healing process.

MAJOR NUTRIENTS PER 6 OYSTERS

Calories	50
Total fat	1.3 g
Protein	4.4 g
Vitamin B$_{12}$	13.6 mcg
Folate	15 mcg
Selenium	53.5 mcg
Magnesium	28 mg
Zinc	31.8 mg
Calcium	37 mg
Iron	4.9 mcg

Did you know?

Traditionally, an oyster is eaten "all in one go" from the shell, without chewing. You can also cook oysters, but some of the beneficial compounds may be lost.

Although there is little scientific evidence that oysters are an aphrodisiac, they are one of our best sources of zinc—and this mineral is strongly linked with fertility and virility. Zinc is also important for skin health and the immune system, and it is an antioxidant. Recent research has found that ceramide compounds in oysters inhibit the growth of breast cancer cells. Oysters also contain reasonable amounts of essential omega-3 fats, are rich in selenium for a healthy immune system, and contain easily absorbed iron for energy and healthy blood.

- Excellent source of zinc for fertility and virility.
- Contain compounds and materials that can protect against cancers.
- High iron content for energy, resistance to infection, and healthy blood.
- A good source of the B vitamins.

Practical tips:
Oysters need to be very fresh and, if eaten raw, they should be alive. It is safest to eat farmed oysters because, in recent years, wild oysters have been found to contain toxic levels of contaminants. To prepare fresh oysters, scrub the shells with a stiff brush under cold water. Discard any that are cracked or damaged, or whose shells do not snap shut when tapped—this means that the oyster inside is dead.

Oysters rockefeller

MAKES 24

24 large live oysters
kosher salt
1 tablespoon unsalted butter
2 tablespoons light olive oil
6 scallions, chopped
1 large garlic clove, crushed
3 tablespoons finely chopped celery
15 watercress sprigs
3 cups young spinach leaves, rinsed and trimmed
1 tablespoon anise-flavored liqueur
¼ cup fresh bread crumbs
few drops of hot pepper sauce, to taste
¼ teaspoon pepper
lemon wedges, to serve

METHOD

1   Preheat the oven to 400°F. Shuck the oysters, running an oyster knife under each oyster to loosen it from its shell. Pour off the liquid. Arrange a ½–¾-inch layer of salt in a roasting pan large enough to hold the oysters in a single layer. Nestle the oyster shells in the salt so that they remain upright. Cover with a damp dish towel and chill while you prepare the topping.

2   Line four plates with a layer of salt deep enough to hold six shells upright on each. Set the plates aside.

3   Melt half the butter and the oil in a large skillet. Add the scallions, garlic, and celery and cook over medium heat, stirring frequently, for 2–3 minutes, or until softened.

4   Stir in the remaining butter, then add the watercress and spinach and cook for 1 minute, or until the leaves wilt. Transfer to a small food processor or blender and add the remaining ingredients. Process until well blended.

5   Spoon 2–3 teaspoons of the sauce over each oyster. Bake in the preheated oven for 20 minutes. Transfer to the prepared plates and serve with lemon wedges for squeezing over the scallops.

31

Kefir

Although kefir is less well known than its cousin yogurt, its rejuvenating, immune-enhancing properties are making it increasingly popular.

MAJOR NUTRIENTS PER ½ CUP / 3½ FL. OZ. KEFIR

Calories	61
Total fat	Varies
Protein	Varies
Carbohydrate	Varies
Calcium	120 mg
Potassium	150 mg
Zinc	0.36 mg

Adding kefir to the diet provides an extra dimension to the immune-supporting actions of fermented foods, such as yogurt, miso, and sauerkraut. It has been shown to have extremely positive effects in the digestive tract, where the balance of good and bad bacteria is the foundation of the body's ability to fight bacterial infection, viruses, and fungal overgrowths. Kefir has also been shown to actively destroy harmful invading bacteria, and is believed to slow the growth of certain tumors. One of the probiotic bacteria alive in kefir, *Lactobacillus casei*, is strong enough to fight off pneumonia.

- Kefir's smaller curds make it easier to digest than yogurt, which helps it in its task of removing toxins via the digestive tract.
- Has all the protein and calcium benefits of milk but is easier to tolerate for people with mild lactose intolerance.
- Traditionally used to boost energy, help relieve skin disorders, and promote longevity.

Practical tips:
You can find kefir at good health food stores, or make it yourself from cultures available on the Internet. Kefir can also be made with coconut water or even just water (although the nutritional values listed on this page include the nutrients of milk). Use kefir as you would yogurt. It makes a great base for smoothies because the sour taste offsets fruit perfectly.

Blueberry smoothie

SERVES 2

½ cup kefir
½ cup water
1 cup blueberries, plus extra to decorate

METHOD

1 Put the kefir, water, and blueberries into a food processor or blender and process until smooth.

2 Pour into glasses and top with whole blueberries.

32

Greek yogurt

Greek yogurt with live cultures contains bacterial cultures that boost the immune system and keep the digestive system healthy and robust.

Greek yogurt contains less sugar and more protein than other yogurts because it is strained to remove the carbohydrate-rich whey. Its thick texture leaves you fuller than more watery versions and the lower level of lactose (milk sugar) it contains makes it easier to digest. Eating yogurt with live cultures regularly has been shown to enhance immune responses and improve resistance to disease.

- All yogurt helps reduce bad cholesterol, but only yogurt with live cultures raises good cholesterol levels, ensuring the arteries stay healthy.
- An important vitamin B12 source for vegetarians, which could help to prevent skin conditions, as well as Alzheimer's disease, heart disease, and diabetes.

Practical tips:
Always choose yogurt with live cultures for the beneficial bacterial cultures. If possible, buy from local farms via health food stores or farmer's markets—these products will have their own natural bacteria instead of bacteria that has been added in the production process. Avoid fruit-flavored yogurt, because it often contains added sugar; instead, sweeten the yogrut with fresh fruit or cinnamon. The creamy, fresh taste of Greek yogurt makes it a good alternative to milk, cream, sour cream, and crème fraîche in main meals and side dishes, as well as some desserts.

MAJOR NUTRIENTS PER ½ CUP/3½ FL. OZ. GREEK YOGURT (WITH LIVE CULTURES)

Calories	61
Total fat	3.25 g
Protein	3.47 g
Carbohydrate	4.66 g
Vitamin A	99 IU
Vitamin B$_2$	0.14 mg
Vitamin B$_5$	0.39 mg
Vitamin B$_{12}$	0.37 mcg
Choline	15.2 mg
Calcium	121 mg
Potassium	155 mg

Tzatzíki

SERVES 4

1 small cucumber
1¼ cups Greek yogurt with live cultures
1 large garlic clove, crushed
1 tablespoon chopped fresh mint or dill
salt and pepper

METHOD

1. Peel and grate the cucumber. Put in a strainer and squeeze out as much of the water as possible. Put the cucumber into a bowl.

2. Add the yogurt, garlic, and chopped mint (reserve a little as a garnish, if desired) to the cucumber and season with pepper. Mix well together and chill in the refrigerator for about 2 hours before serving.

3. Stir the dip and transfer to a serving bowl. Sprinkle with salt and serve.

33

Eggs

Eggs are an excellent source of protein, and they also contain all of the amino acids necessary for the body to repair and regenerate cells.

Eggs are ideally packaged to support new life, and so contain all the nutrients we need for growth: iron, zinc, vitamin A, vitamin D, the B vitamins, and omega-3 fats. Many people avoid them because of their high cholesterol content, but the body can regulate this if the diet is generally low in sugar and saturated fat. Many studies show that egg consumption helps prevent chronic age-related conditions, such as coronary heart disease, loss of muscle mass, eye degeneration, hearing loss, and memory loss.

- Contain vitamin B_{12} to help combat fatigue, depression, and lethargy.
- Vitamin A and lutein ensure eye protection and continuing good sight.
- One of the few dietary sources of both vitamins K and D, which work together to keep bones strong.
- Contain sulfur and lecithin, substances that help the liver with digestion and detoxification.

Practical tips:
Eggs are a truly useful staple food—they can be cooked in many different ways, including poaching, scrambling, and boiling. Omelets or frittatas, loaded with healthy vegetables, can also be eaten cold as a snack. Buy organic eggs from pasture-raised chickens because their feed gives these eggs higher nutritional value, indicated by their deeper yellow yolk and richer taste.

MAJOR NUTRIENTS PER MEDIUM EGG

Calories	65
Total fat	4.37 g
Omega-3 oils	32.6 mg
Omega-6 oils	505 mg
Omega-9 oils	1,582 mg
Protein	5.53 g
Carbohydrate	0.34 g
Vitamin A	214 IU
Vitamin D	22 IU
Vitamin B_2	0.21 mg
Vitamin B_5	0.63 mg
Vitamin B_{12}	0.57 mcg
Vitamin K	0.1 mcg
Choline	110.5 mg
Iron	0.81 mg
Selenium	13.9 mcg
Zinc	0.49 mg
Lutein/Zeaxanthin	146 mcg

Mixed herb omelet

SERVES 1

2 extra-large eggs
2 tablespoons milk
3 tablespoons butter
leaves from 1 fresh parsley
sprig, chopped
2 fresh chives, chopped
salt and pepper
fresh salad greens, to serve

METHOD

1 Break the eggs into a bowl. Add the milk and season with salt and pepper, then quickly beat until just blended.
2 Heat a skillet over medium–high heat until hot. Add 2 tablespoons of the butter and use a spatula to rub it over the bottom and around the side of the skillet as it melts.
3 As soon as the butter stops sizzling, pour in the eggs. Use the spatula to stir the eggs around the skillet in a circular motion. Do not scrape the bottom of the skillet.
4 As the omelet begins to set, use the spatula to push the cooked egg toward the center of the skillet. Continue doing this for 3 minutes, or until the omelet looks set on the bottom but is still slightly runny on top.
5 Put the chopped herbs in the center of the omelet. Use the spatula to fold the omelet in half, over the herbs. Slide onto a plate, then rub the remaining butter over the top. Serve immediately, accompanied by fresh salad greens.

34

Brown rice

The high fiber content of brown rice can help to lower blood cholesterol levels and keep blood sugar levels even, making it a healthier choice than white rice.

MAJOR NUTRIENTS PER ⅓ CUP/2½ OZ. BROWN RICE, UNCOOKED

Calories	222
Total fat	1.8 g
Protein	5 g
Carbohydrate	46 g
Fiber	3.6 g
Niacin	3 mg
Vitamin B$_1$	0.2 mg
Vitamin B$_6$	0.3 mg
Selenium	19.6 mcg
Magnesium	86 mg
Iron	0.8 mg
Zinc	1.3 g
Calcium	20 mg

Did you know?

Ninety per cent of all rice is still grown and consumed in Asia, where it has been eaten for over 6,000 years.

While white rice contains few nutrients other than starch, brown rice has several nutritional benefits. Regular consumption of brown rice and other whole grains has been shown to help prevent heart disease, diabetes, and some cancers. It is a good source of fiber, which can help reduce cholesterol levels in the blood and keep blood sugar levels even. Brown rice also contains some protein, and is a good source of several of the B vitamins and of minerals, particularly selenium and magnesium.

- A reasonably low glycemic index (GI) food that can help control blood sugar levels and may be helpful for diabetics.
- Useful B vitamin content to help convert food into energy and keep the nervous system healthy.
- High selenium content may help protect against cancers, and high magnesium content is important for a healthy heart.

Practical tips:
Store rice in a cool, dark cupboard and use within a few months of purchase. Brown rice tends not to keep as well as white rice because it contains small amounts of fat, which can spoil over time. It's also worth noting that the longer you store raw rice, the longer it may take to cook. Leftover cooked rice can be kept for a day or two in a refrigerator if you cool it quickly, but it must be reheated until piping hot before serving to kill bacteria that can cause food poisoning.

Brown rice vegetable pilaf

SERVES 4

¼ cup vegetable oil

1 red onion, finely chopped

2 celery stalks, leaves included, diced

2 carrots, peeled and shredded

1 fresh green chile, seeded and finely chopped

3 scallions, finely chopped

⅓ cup whole almonds, sliced lengthwise

2½ cups cold, cooked brown rice

¾ cup cold, cooked split red lentils

¾ cup vegetable stock

⅓ cup fresh orange juice

salt and pepper

METHOD

1 Heat 2 tablespoons of the oil in deep skillet with a lid. Add the onion and cook over medium heat for 5 minutes, or until softened.

2 Add the celery, carrots, chile, scallions, and almonds and stir-fry for 2 minutes, or until the vegetables are tender but still firm to the bite. Transfer to a bowl and set aside until needed.

3 Add the remaining oil to the skillet. Stir in the rice and lentils and cook over medium–high heat, stirring, for 1–2 minutes, or until heated through. Reduce the heat and stir in the stock and orange juice. Season with salt and pepper.

4 Return the vegetables to the skillet. Toss with the rice for a few minutes until heated through. Transfer to a warm serving dish and serve.

35

Kidney beans

Iron-rich kidney beans are an excellent source of good-quality protein, zinc, and fiber, and they contain compounds to help prevent blood clots.

Kidney beans are invaluable for vegetarians because they are high in good-quality protein and minerals. A ⅓ cup/2¼-ounce portion of kidney beans contains at least one-quarter of our day's iron needs to help prevent anemia and increase energy levels, while their good zinc content helps boost the immune system and maintain fertility. The high degree of insoluble fiber in kidney beans helps prevent colon cancer, while for diabetics and people with insulin resistance, the total fiber content helps to regulate blood sugar levels.

- Excellent source of protein, iron, and calcium for vegetarians.
- Very high fiber content helps regulate release of insulin and helps to prevent hunger—a good choice for dieters.
- Protects against colon cancer.
- Extremely high in potassium, which can minimize fluid retention and may help control high blood pressure.

Practical tips:
There is little nutritional difference between cooked dried kidney beans and canned kidney beans, so, if you don't have much time, use canned beans. Raw kidney beans contain a toxin that can cause an upset stomach, vomiting, and diarrhea if not cooked correctly. When using dried beans, they must be soaked overnight, or for at least 12 hours, and then rinsed in fresh cold water before being rapidly boiled for at least 10 minutes before cooking to remove the toxins.

MAJOR NUTRIENTS PER ⅓ CUP/2¼ OZ. DRIED RED KIDNEY BEANS

Calories	200
Total fat	0.8 g
Protein	13.7 g
Carbohydrate	36 g
Fiber	10 g
Folate	205 mcg
Vitamin B$_1$	0.25 mg
Niacin	0.9 mg
Magnesium	66 mg
Potassium	640 mg
Zinc	1.6 g
Calcium	55 mg
Iron	3.5 mg

Vegetarian chili

SERVES 6

METHOD

¼ cup olive oil

2 cups small white button mushrooms

1 large onion, chopped

1 garlic clove, chopped

1 green bell pepper, seeded and cut into strips

1 teaspoon each paprika, ground coriander, and ground cumin

¼–½ teaspoon chili powder

1 (14½-ounce) can diced tomatoes

⅔ cup vegetable stock

1 tablespoon tomato paste

1 (15-ounce) cand red kidney beans, drained rinsed

salt and pepper

2 tablespoons chopped fresh cilantro, to garnish

cooked rice and sour cream, to serve

1   Heat 1 tablespoon of the oil in a large skillet. Add the mushrooms and stir-fry until golden. Remove them with a slotted spoon and set aside until needed.

2   Add the remaining oil to the skillet. Add the onion, garlic, and green bell pepper and stir-fry for 5 minutes. Stir in the paprika, coriander, cumin, and chili powder and cook for an additional 1 minute.

3   Add the tomatoes, stock, and tomato paste, stir well, then cover and cook for 20 minutes.

4   Add the reserved mushrooms and kidney beans and cook, covered, for an additional 20 minutes. Season with salt and pepper. Garnish with the cilantro and serve with cooked rice and sour cream.

36

Lentils

Small, lens-shaped dried lentils are one of the beans richest in cancer-blocking fibers called isoflavones and lignan, and they are low in fat and saturates.

Lentils come in a variety of colors and include green, brown, and red. Green and brown lentils tend to contain the highest levels of nutrients and fiber. Lentils are a rich source of fiber, both insoluble and soluble, which helps protect us against cancer and cardiovascular disease. They also contain plant chemicals called isoflavones, which may offer protection from cancer and coronary heart disease, and lignan, which has a mild estrogen-like effect that may lower the risk of cancer, minimize premenstrual syndrome, and protect against osteoporosis. Lentils are also rich in the B vitamins, folate, and all major minerals, particularly iron and zinc.

- Rich in fiber for protection from cardiovascular disease and cancers.
- High iron content for healthy blood and energy levels.
- Contain plant chemicals to help premenstrual syndrome and bone health.
- High zinc content to boost the immune system.

MAJOR NUTRIENTS PER ⅓ CUP/2¼ OZ. DRIED GREEN LENTILS

Calories	212
Total fat	0.6 g
Protein	15.5 g
Carbohydrate	36 g
Fiber	18 g
Folate	287 mcg
Vitamin B$_1$	0.5 mg
Niacin	1.6 mg
Vitamin B$_6$	0.3 mg
Magnesium	73 mg
Potassium	573 mg
Zinc	2.9 g
Calcium	34 mg
Iron	4.5 mg

Did you know?

Lentils are thought to be one of the earliest foods to have been cultivated, with 8,000-year-old seeds found at sites in the Middle East.

Practical tips:
Lentils are one of the few dried beans that don't need soaking before cooking. They are also relatively quick to cook, and will take approximately 30 minutes in simmering water. Cooking dried lentils in stock makes a simple, healthy base for a soup, which can be added to as desired. Canned lentils have almost as many nutrients as dried ones so are a convenient alternative.

Five-spice lentil stew

SERVES 4

⅔ cup dried red split lentils

⅔ cup dried peeled, split mung beans

3¾ cups hot water

1 teaspoon ground turmeric

1 teaspoon salt, or to taste

1 tablespoon lemon juice

2 tablespoons sunflower oil or olive oil

¼ teaspoon black mustard seeds

¼ teaspoon cumin seeds

¼ teaspoon nigella seeds

¼ teaspoon fennel seeds

4–5 fenugreek seeds

2–3 crushed red pepper

1 small tomato, seeded and cut into strips and fresh cilantro sprigs, to garnish

naan, to serve

METHOD

1 Rinse the lentils and mung beans under cold running water, then place in a saucepan with the hot water and bring to a boil. Reduce the heat and simmer for 5–6 minutes. Add the turmeric, reduce the heat to low, cover, and cook for an additional 20 minutes. Add the salt, lemon juice, and a little more water, if the mixture is too thick.

2 Heat the oil in a small saucepan over medium heat. When hot, but not smoking, add the mustard seeds. As soon as they begin to pop, reduce the heat to low and add the cumin seeds, nigella seeds, fennel seeds, fenugreek seeds, and crushed red pepper. Let the spices sizzle until the seeds begin to pop and the crushed pepper has blackened.

3 Transfer to a serving dish and pour the contents of the saucepan over the lentils. Garnish with the tomato strips and cilantro sprigs. Serve with naan.

37

Pot barley

This extremely nutritious starchy grain contains soluble fiber, which helps to lower bad blood cholesterol and protects from hormonal cancers and heart disease.

MAJOR NUTRIENTS PER ⅓ CUP/2¼ OZ. POT BARLEY, UNCOOKED

Calories	212
Total fat	1.4 g
Protein	7.5 g
Carbohydrate	44 g
Fiber	10.4 g
Vitamin B₁	0.4 mg
Niacin	2.8 mg
Selenium	22.5 mcg
Magnesium	80 mg
Potassium	271 mg
Zinc	1.7 g
Calcium	20 mg
Iron	2.2 mg
Lutein/Zeaxanthin	96 mcg

Pot barley is a grain with a rich, slightly nutty flavor and a chewy texture. Most barley that is sold is pearl barley, which has had almost all of the nutrients and fiber removed by processing, whereas pot barley has been polished so only the hull has been removed and is, therefore, a good source of nutrients. These include a fiberlike compound called lignan, which may protect against breast and other hormone-dependent cancers, as well as heart disease. Unusually for a grain, barley contains lutein and zeaxanthin, both of which help to protect eyesight and eye health.

- Whole grain that protects against cancers and heart disease.
- A good source of minerals and the B vitamins.
- High in fiber to keep the colon healthy and soluble fiber to lower blood cholesterol.
- Helps to keep eyes healthy.

Practical tips:
Pot barley needs up to two hours of simmering in water, but presoaking it for several hours will shorten the cooking time. The fats in barley can make it spoil after a short time, especially if kept in warm, light conditions, so store barley in a cool, dry, dark place in an airtight container and use within two to three months. Barley water, made by steeping the grains in water, has long been considered a health drink for its diuretic and kidney-supporting effect.

Hearty barley vegetable soup

SERVES 6–4

2 tablespoons sunflower oil

1 onion, finely chopped

1 celery stalk, finely chopped

1 garlic clove, crushed

6½ cups vegetable stock or water

½ cup pot barley, rinsed

1 bouquet garni, made with 1 bay leaf, fresh thyme sprigs, and fresh parsley sprigs tied together

2 carrots, peeled and diced

1 (14½-ounce) can diced tomatoes

pinch of sugar

½ head cabbage, cored and shredded

salt and pepper

2 tablespoons chopped fresh parsley, to garnish

METHOD

1   Heat the oil in a large saucepan. Add the onion, celery, and garlic and cook over medium heat for 5–7 minutes, or until softened.

2   Pour in the stock and bring to a boil, skimming off any foam that rises to the surface with a slotted spoon. Add the barley and bouquet garni, reduce the heat to low, cover, and simmer for 30 minutes–1 hour, or until the grains are just beginning to soften.

3   Add the carrots, tomatoes with their can juices, and the sugar to the pan. Bring the liquid back to a boil, then reduce the heat to low, cover, and simmer for an additional 30 minutes, or until the barley and carrots are tender.

4   Just before serving, remove the bouquet garni, stir in the cabbage, and season with salt and pepper. Cook until the cabbage wilts, then ladle into warm soup bowls, garnish with parsley, and serve immediately.

38

Oats

Economical oats are high in soluble fiber and a source of healthy fats. They can keep hunger at bay, lower bad cholesterol, and keep blood sugar levels even.

MAJOR NUTRIENTS PER ⅓ CUP/2¼ OZ. OATS, UNCOOKED

Calories	233
Total fat	4 g
Protein	10 g
Carbohydrate	40 g
Fiber	6.4 g
Folate	34 mcg
Vitamin B$_1$	0.5 mg
Niacin	0.6 mg
Vitamin E	1.5 mg
Magnesium	106 mg
Potassium	257 mg
Zinc	2.4 g
Calcium	32 mg
Iron	2.8 mg

Oats have several health-giving properties. They are rich in the soluble fiber beta-glucan and have been proven to help lower bad cholesterol, boost good cholesterol, and maintain a healthy circulatory system. Oats also contain a range of antioxidants and plant chemicals to help keep heart and arteries healthy, such as avenanthramides (a phytoalexin plant chemical with antibiotic properties) and vitamin E. They also contain polyphenols, plant compounds that can suppress tumor growth. They are relatively low on the glycemic index (GI), which means they are a particularly useful food for dieters, people with insulin resistance, and diabetics.

• Contain plant chemicals to help reduce the risk of cancers.
• A good source of a wide range of vitamins and minerals, including the B vitamins, vitamin E, magnesium, calcium, and iron.

Practical tips:
Keep oats in an airtight container in a cool, dry, dark place and use within two to three weeks. Oat flakes can be used for making cookies and crisp toppings, and oat flour can replace wheat flour. Although oats do contain small amounts of gluten, people with gluten intolerance often find they can tolerate oats in their diet, especially if limited to no more than 1⅓ cups a day. People withi celiac should check with their physician before eating oats.

Honey & oat bars

MAKES 16

1½ sticks unsalted butter, plus extra for greasing

3 tablespoons honey

¾ cup demerara sugar or other raw sugar

⅓ cup smooth peanut butter

2½ cups rolled oats

⅓ cup chopped dried apricots

2 tablespoons sunflower seeds

2 tablespoons sesame seeds

METHOD

1   Preheat the oven to 350°F. Grease and line an 8-inch square baking pan.

2   Melt the butter, honey, and sugar in a saucepan over low heat. When the butter has melted, add the peanut butter and stir until everything is well combined. Add all the remaining ingredients and mix well.

3   Press the mixture into the prepared pan and bake in the preheated oven for 20 minutes. Remove from the oven and let cool in the pan, then cut into squares and serve.

39

Quinoa

The best source of complete protein in the plant kingdom, quinoa provides all the necessary building blocks for skin, bone, and brain regeneration.

Most plant foods are lacking in one or more of the essential amino acids, but quinoa is an easy one-food solution, containing all the essential amino acids, plus a good range of minerals and the B vitamins. These enable the protein content of quinoa to be used effectively, so that it can provide the vast amount of energy needed for the constant renewal of skin, hair, nails, teeth, bone, and organs. Quinoa is actually a seed, not a grain. As such, it is high in anti-inflammatory omega-6 oils and is ideal for those people who cannot tolerate wheat or gluten.

- Contains phosphorus to make phospholipids in the brain and nervous system.
- Potassium balances out sodium, reducing bloating, puffiness, and high blood pressure.
- Zinc and selenium offer potent antioxidant protection.

Practical tips:
Stored correctly, quinoa will last for up to a year in an airtight container. Keep in a cool, dry, dark place for best results. Cook quinoa in a similar way to rice. It has a pleasant, nutty flavor, and is delicious in Mexican and Indian meals. You can also make a great hot quinoa, either from flakes or from the grain itself. Quinoa is versatile enough to be cooked in both sweet desserts and unsweetened dishes.

MAJOR NUTRIENTS PER ½ CUP/3½ OZ. QUINOA, UNCOOKED

Calories	368
Total fat	6.07 g
Omega-6 oils	2,977 mg
Protein	14.12 g
Carbohydrate	64.16 g
Fiber	7 mg
Vitamin B_1	0.36 mg
Vitamin B_2	0.32 mg
Vitamin B_3	1.52 mg
Vitamin B_5	0.77 mg
Vitamin B_6	0.49 mg
Folate	184 mg
Magnesium	197 mg
Iron	4.57 mg
Phosphorus	457 mg
Potassium	563 mg
Manganese	2.03 mg
Selenium	8.5 mcg
Zinc	3.1 mg

Tabbouleh

SERVES 4

1½ cups quinoa

2½ cups water

10 vine-ripened cherry tomatoes, halved

3-inch piece cucumber, quartered and sliced

3 scallions, finely chopped

juice of ½ lemon

2 tablespoons extra virgin olive oil

¼ cup chopped fresh mint

¼ cup chopped fresh cilantro

¼ cup chopped fresh parsley

salt and pepper

METHOD

1. Put the quinoa into medium saucepan and cover with the water. Bring to a boil, then reduce the heat, cover, and simmer over low heat for 15 minutes. Drain if necessary.
2. Let the quinoa cool slightly before combining with the remaining ingredients in a salad bowl. Adjust the seasoning, if necessary, before serving.

40

Buckwheat

Buckwheat contains a rich supply of flavonoids, particularly rutin. These help to keep blood circulation flowing freely and prevent varicose veins.

Buckwheat is technically a seed, not a grain, so it is an excellent source of fiber and energy for people who are intolerant to wheat and gluten. Whether you have an intolerance or not, reducing your wheat intake could be beneficial—buckwheat is easier to digest than wheat and also more alkalizing, meaning that it helps the body's physical processes work more efficiently. It is a particularly sustaining energy source and is recommended for diabetics, because it releases its sugars slowly into the bloodstream. Buckwheat, like millet, also contains substances called nutrilosides that are essential in detoxification processes, helping rid the body of harmful, aging toxins.

- Contains lecithin, which helps break down fats in the liver and in the food that you eat, aiding detoxification and reducing cravings for fatty foods.
- Magnesium and potassium work together to ensure a healthy heart and strong bones.
- Selenium produces both of the rejuvenating antioxidants glutathione and coenzyme Q-10.

Practical tips:
Buckwheat may be used as an alternative to rice. It can also be bought in flakes and served as a hot breakfast cereal. Buckwheat flour makes excellent gluten-free pancakes, which are traditional in Poland and Russia, and also eaten in France.

MAJOR NUTRIENTS PER ½ CUP/3½ OZ. BUCKWHEAT, UNCOOKED

Calories	343
Total fat	3.4 g
Omega-6 oils	1,052 mg
Protein	13.25 g
Carbohydrate	71.5 g
Fiber	10 mg
Vitamin B_2	0.43 mg
Vitamin B_3	7.02 mg
Vitamin B_5	1.23 mg
Vitamin B_6	0.21 mg
Folate	30 mcg
Magnesium	231 mg
Potassium	460 mg
Manganese	1.33 mg
Selenium	8.3 mcg
Zinc	2.4 mcg

Buckwheat, feta & tomato salad

SERVES 4

2 tablespoons olive oil
1 onion, chopped
2 garlic cloves, crushed
1 cup buckwheat groats
1 (14½-ounce) can
diced tomatoes
½ teaspoon tomato paste
1 cup low-sodium
vegetable stock
1 tablespoon chopped
fresh sage, or 1 teaspoon
dried sage
pinch of crushed red pepper
¾ cup crumbled, drained
feta cheese
salt and pepper

METHOD

1   Heat the oil in a deep skillet with a tight-fitting lid over medium–high heat. Add the onion and garlic and sauté for 5 minutes. Add the buckwheat and sauté for an additional 1 minute.

2   Add the tomatoes with their can juices, the tomato paste, stock, sage, and crushed red pepper and season with salt and pepper. Bring to a boil, stirring continuously, then reduce the heat to low, cover the pan, and let simmer for 20–25 minutes, or until the liquid has been absorbed and the buckwheat is tender.

3   Lightly stir in the feta cheese, replace the lid, and let the buckwheat stand for up to 20 minutes. Just before serving, lightly stir with a fork.

41

Miso

Miso is a traditional Japanese ingredient used as a seasoning in dishes—the Japanese diet has long been associated with long life and good health.

Miso is a traditional Japanese seasoning, most often produced by fermenting soybeans with salt and koji yeast mold, although it can also be made with rice, wheat, or barley. Like yogurt and kefir, miso is associated with good digestive health, because it feeds the beneficial probiotic bacteria present in the body. This supports toxin elimination and the absorption of nutrients to keep the body healthy. Fermented foods also help the immune system, helping to reduce multiple sensitivities and inflammation, as seen in hay fever and skin problems.

- Contains tryptophan, needed for serotonin production, which encourages good mood and restorative sleep.
- Manganese makes the detoxifying antioxidant enzyme superoxide dismutase.
- Vitamin K transports calcium around the body in support of good bone health and efficient blood clotting.
- Zinc-rich food that promotes optimal immune function and rapid healing, helping your skin look more youthful.

Practical tips:
Miso is salty, but a little goes a long way in terms of taste and mineral content. The paste is superior to the powdered form and can be used to make an instant, simple soup when mixed with boiling water. Add miso to boiled vegetables and ginger to make a heartier broth, which you can supplement with shrimp, chicken, or tofu.

MAJOR NUTRIENTS PER 1 TABLESPOON MISO

Calories	34
Total fat	1.03 g
Protein	2.01 g
Carbohydrate	4.55 g
Fiber	0.93 g
Vitamin B_1	0.02 mg
Vitamin B_2	0.04 mg
Vitamin B_3	0.16 mg
Vitamin B_5	0.06 mg
Vitamin B_6	0.03 mg
Vitamin B_{12}	0.43 mcg
Vitamin K	8.53 mcg
Iron	0.43 mg
Selenium	1.2 mcg
Zinc	0.44 mg
Manganese	0.3 mg

Miso soup

SERVES 4

4 cups water
2 teaspoons dashi granules
¾ cup diced, drained
silken tofu
4 shiitake mushrooms,
finely sliced
¼ cup miso paste
2 scallions, chopped

METHOD

1   Put the water in a large saucepan with the dashi granules and
bring to a boil. Add the tofu and mushrooms, reduce the heat,
and let simmer for 3 minutes.

2   Stir in the miso paste and let simmer gently, stirring, until the
miso has dissolved.

3   Add the scallions and serve immediately. If you let the soup
stand, the miso will settle, so stir before serving to recombine.

42

Honey

Raw honey is one of nature's oldest known antibacterial products. Used topically, honey has an antiseptic and antibacterial effect.

Honey is created when the saliva of bees meets the nectar they collect from flowers, so the properties of a particular honey will reflect those of the flowers the bees have visited most prominently. In its raw state, it contains an array of antioxidants, such as chrysin and vitamin C, but these properties are destroyed when it is excessively heated or processed. Manuka honey from New Zealand is the only honey that has been tested for its ability to destroy harmful bacteria, and batches of this are given a Unique Manuka Factor (UMF) according to strength. Manuka has been shown to be twice as effective as other honeys against *E. coli* and *Staphylococcus* bacteria, which commonly infect wounds.

- Raw honey contains propolis, which helps reduce inflammation and premature aging.
- Good-quality honey contains probiotic benefical bacteria *lactobacilli* and *bifidobacteria* to support immunity.
- When applied to the skin, it has been shown to help heal pimples, burns, cuts, and sores.

Practical tips:
Choose good-quality honey—look for local, raw, and unprocessed varieties from farm shops. Darker types, such as buckwheat and sage, contain the most antioxidants, and the honey produced by flower-fed bees in the summer contains more beneficial bacteria.

**MAJOR NUTRIENTS PER
1 TABLESPOON HONEY**

Calories	45.5
Total fat	0 g
Protein	0.04 g
Carbohydrate	12.36 g
Fiber	0.03 g

Did you know?

When mixed with water, honey creates antiseptic hydrogen peroxide, which can be applied directly to wounds to dry them out and keep them free from infection while they heal.

Homemade granola

SERVES 6–8

2¾ cups rolled oats

2 Granny Smith or other tart apples, peeled and diced

½ cup chopped dried figs

½ cup slivered almonds

2 tablespoons good-quality honey

¼ cup cold water

1 teaspoon ground cinnamon

1 teaspoon vanilla extract

1 teaspoon butter, melted, for greasing

Greek yogurt with live cultures, to serve

METHOD

1   Preheat the oven to 325°F. Mix together the oats, apples, figs, and almonds in a large bowl. Bring the honey, water, cinnamon, and vanilla extract to a boil in a saucepan, then pour over the oat mixture, stirring well to make sure that all the ingredients are coated.

2   Lightly grease a large baking pan with the butter and spread the oat mixture out evenly in the pan. Bake for 40–45 minutes, or until the granola is golden brown, stirring with a fork from time to time to break up any lumps. Pour into a clean baking pan and let cool before storing in an airtight container. Serve sprinkled over bowls of Greek yogurt.

43

Cinnamon

Cinnamon is an anti-inflammatory, antibacterial spice that can help relieve bloating and heartburn, and it offers protection against strokes.

MAJOR NUTRIENTS PER 2 TABLESPOONS / ½ OZ. CINNAMON

Calories	18
Total fat	Trace
Protein	Trace
Carbohydrate	5.5 g
Fiber	3.7 g
Folate	287 mcg
Potassium	34 mg
Calcium	84 mg
Iron	2.6 mg

Cinnamon contains several oils and compounds, including cinnamaldehyde, cinnamyl acetate, and cinnamyl alcohol, which have a variety of beneficial actions. Cinnamaldehyde has an anticoagulant action, meaning that it can help to protect against strokes, and is also anti-inflammatory, relieving symptoms of arthritis and asthma. The spice is a digestive aid, relieving bloating and flatulence, and it can reduce the discomfort of heartburn. Cinnamon has antibacterial action that can block the yeast fungus *candida* and bugs that can cause food poisoning. In one study, cinnamon was shown to lower blood sugars and blood cholesterol.

- Helps to combat indigestion and bloating.
- Antibacterial and antifungal.
- Helps prevent blood clots.
- May lower bad cholesterol and blood sugars.

Practical tips:
True cinnamon is the inner bark of an evergreen tree of the laurel family native to Sri Lanka, and cassia is another variety native to China. Both are widely available, but it is not always possible to know which one you are buying. Whole bark cinnamon sticks will retain their flavor and aroma for up to a year, while the ground dried spice will last for about six months. Whole or pieces of cinammon sticks and ground cinnamon, can be used to flavor both sweet and unsweetened dishes.

Broiled cinnamon oranges

SERVES 4

4 large oranges
1 teaspoon ground cinnamon
1 tablespoon demerara sugar
or other raw sugar

METHOD

1 Preheat the broiler to high. Cut the oranges in half and discard any seeds. Using a sharp or curved grapefruit knife, carefully cut the flesh away from the skin by cutting around the edge of the fruit. Cut across the segments to loosen the flesh into bite-size pieces that will then spoon out easily.

2 Arrange the orange halves, cut side up, in a shallow, ovenproof dish. Mix together the cinnamon and sugar in a small bowl and sprinkle the mixture evenly over the orange halves.

3 Cook under the preheated broiler for 3–5 minutes, or until the sugar has caramelized and is golden and bubbling. Serve immediately.

44

Green tea

The Chinese and Japanese have long understood the health attributes of green tea, and they view it as an important way to care for their heart, energy, and skin.

MAJOR NUTRIENTS PER 1 CUP/8 FL OZ. GREEN TEA

Calories	2
Total fat	0 g
Protein	0 g
Carbohydrate	Trace
Fiber	0 g
Catechins	3.75 g

The leaves of the tea plant *Camellia sinensis* are loaded with catechins, which have been found to have natural antioxidant, antibacterial, and antiviral properties, thereby protecting against cancer and helping to lower cholesterol and regulate blood clotting. One such compound, epigallocatechin gallate (EGCG), is able to penetrate the cells and protect the crucial DNA that the body relies on to replicate cells and combat the damage caused by aging. EGCG also prevents cancer cells from forming and can help reduce the severity of allergies by blocking the body's response.

• May act as a weight loss aid by helping to burn fat and regulate blood sugar and insulin levels.
• Contains quercetin, a bioflavonoid (plant chemical) that reduces inflammation and helps control food allergies.
• Catechins promote liver detoxification, so assisting in the removal of aging toxins and promoting glowing skin.

Practical tips:
Changing from black tea or coffee to green tea will lower your intake of caffeine and its aging effects. Green tea leaves are the dried leaves of the tea plant, while black, "normal" tea is fermented. The fermentation process makes black tea much higher in caffeine: about 50 mg a cup compared to 5 mg for green tea. Different varieties have different strengths and taste, so it's advisable to experiment to find the one you enjoy most.

Green tea & yellow plum smoothie

SERVES 2   METHOD

1 green tea bag
1¼ cups boiling water
1 teaspoon good-quality honey, or to taste (optional)
2 ripe yellow plums, halved and pitted

1 Put the tea bag in a teapot or heatproof bowl and pour over the boiling water. Let steep for 7 minutes. Remove and discard the tea bag. Let cool, then chill in the refrigerator.

2 Pour the chilled tea into a food processor or blender. Add the honey, if using, and plums, and process until smooth.

3 Serve at once.

45

Red wine

Red wine is an important contributor to the age-defying Mediterranean diet. Enjoyed in moderation, it offers excellent heart-protecting properties.

MAJOR NUTRIENTS PER ½ CUP/4 FL OZ. RED WINE

Calories	95
Total fat	0 g
Protein	0.07 g
Carbohydrate	2.87 g
Fiber	Trace
Vitamin C	Trace
Potassium	Trace
Lycopene	Trace
Lutein/Zeaxanthin	145.6 mg

Did you know?

Sipping red wine slowly may increase the blood levels of resveratrol by 100 times, because it is absorbed much better through the mouth than the digestive tract.

The high antioxidant action of red wine comes from a substance called resveratrol, which is found in red grape skins in much higher amounts than in any other food. The major action of resveratrol means that drinking red wine regularly in moderation—less than 5 fluid ounces a day—can make blood platelets less sticky and help blood vessels stay open and flexible. These are both important considerations in regulating blood pressure and, therefore, cutting the risk of heart disease. Drinking red wine has been estimated to add a year to life expectancy, especially if only drunk with food and alongside a healthy diet.

- Resveratrol is an effective agent in disease prevention.
- It has also been shown to have a potent anti-inflammatory action, supporting healthy skin and trouble-free joints.
- Cabernet Sauvignon, in particular, has been shown to help improve the memory deterioration shown in Alzheimer's disease.

Practical tips:
Straying above the recommended a glass a day for women and two glasses a day for men soon negates the benefits of red wine. Quality is also key: the deeper the red, the higher the antioxidant count. The greatest amounts are found in Merlot, Cabernet Sauvignon, and Chianti grapes. Rioja and Pinot Noir offer moderate amounts, while the least benefit is derived from Côtes du Rhône.

Red wine-spiced red cabbage

SERVES 6

2 tablespoons butter

1 garlic clove, chopped

1 head red cabbage, shredded

1 cup golden raisins

1 tablespoon good-quality honey

½ cup red wine

½ cup water

METHOD

1 Melt the butter in a large saucepan over medium heat. Add the garlic and cook, stirring, for 1 minute, until slightly softened.

2 Add the cabbage and golden raisins, then stir in the honey. Cook for an additional 1 minute.

3 Pour in the wine and water and bring to a boil. Reduce the heat, cover, and simmer gently, stirring occasionally, for 45 minutes, or until the cabbage is cooked. Serve hot.

46

Dark chocolate

Our love affair with chocolate is rooted in its health-giving properties. The cacao bean is loaded with nutrients, mood-enhancing chemicals, and antioxidants.

The bean from which we make our favorite confectionery is highly nutricious; it's packed full of rejuvenating potassium, magnesium, vitamins B_3 and B_5, zinc, and selenium. However, its true potency comes from its high antioxidant content. Chocolate contains more than four times the catechins present in green tea and twice as much as in red wine. These substances lower the risk of both heart attacks and cancer by reducing inflammation and helping renew blood vessels, skin, and bone. More immediately, eating dark chocolate releases our beta-endorphins, or "happy chemicals."

- Caffeine and theobromine can boost energy and, in moderation, help to balance blood sugar levels.
- Contains healthy monounsaturated fats, shown to keep the heart youthful and strong.

MAJOR NUTRIENTS PER 3½ OZ. DARK CHOCOLATE (70–85 PERCENT COCOA SOLIDS)

Calories	598
Total fat	42.63 g
Omega-9 oils	12,652 mg
Protein	7.79 g
Carbohydrate	45.9 g
Fiber	10.9 g
Vitamin B_3	1.05 mg
Vitamin B_5	0.42 mg
Magnesium	228 mg
Potassium	716 mg
Phosphorus	308 mg
Iron	11.9 mg
Manganese	1.95 mg
Selenium	6.8 mcg
Zinc	3.31 mg
Caffeine	75.6 mg
Theobromine	448.8 mg

Practical tips:
The health benefits only apply to good-quality dark chocolate—the milk and sugar in milk chocolate negate these. Eating dark chocolate with at least 70 percent cocoa solids will raise your antioxidant levels. Remember that chocolate also has high caffeine content—an average small bar of chocolate contains the equivalent amount of caffeine of one-third of a cup of coffee.

Mole sauce

SERVES 6–8

9 mixed chiles, soaked in hot water for 30 minutes and drained

1 onion, sliced

2–3 garlic cloves, crushed

½ cup sesame seeds

¾ cup toasted slivered almonds

1 teaspoon ground coriander

4 cloves

½ teaspoon pepper

2–3 tablespoons olive oil

1¼ cups chicken stock or vegetable stock

4 ripe tomatoes, peeled and chopped

2 teaspoon ground cinnamon

⅓ cup raisins

¾ cup pumpkin seeds

2 ounces dark chocolate (70 percent minimum cocoa solids), broken into pieces

1 tablespoon red wine vinegar

METHOD

1 Put the chiles into a blender with the onion, garlic, sesame seeds, almonds, coriander, cloves, and pepper and process to form a thick paste.

2 Heat the oil in a saucepan, add the paste, and cook for 5 minutes. Add the stock, tomatoes, cinnamon, raisins, and pumpkin seeds. Bring to a boil, reduce the heat, and simmer, stirring occasionally, for 15 minutes.

3 Add the chocolate and vinegar to the sauce. Cook gently for 5 minutes, then use as required. It is usually served with poultry.

Walnuts

Known for their unusually high content of omega-3 fats, the nutrients in walnuts can help prevent heart disease, cancers, arthritis, and common skin complaints.

MAJOR NUTRIENTS PER ¼ CUP/1¼ OZ. WALNUTS

Calories	196
Total fat	19.5 g
Protein	4.5 g
Carbohydrate	4 g
Fiber	2 g
Niacin	0.3 mg
Vitamin B₆	0.16 mg
Calcium	29 mg
Potassium	132 mg
Magnesium	47 mg
Iron	0.9 mg
Zinc	0.9 mg

Unlike most nuts, walnuts are much richer in polyunsaturated fats than in monounsaturates. The type of polyunsaturates that walnuts contain is mostly the essential omega-3 fats, in the form of alpha-linolenic acid—just one portion will provide you with more than a day's recommended intake. An adequate and balanced intake of the omega fats has been linked with protection from cardiovascular disease, cancers, arthritis, skin problems, and diseases of the nervous system. For people who don't eat fish and fish oils, an intake of omega-3 fats from other sources, such as walnuts, flaxseeds, and soybeans, is important.

• Good source of fiber and the B vitamins.
• Rich in omega-3 fats and antioxidants.
• Good source of a range of important minerals.
• Can lower bad cholesterol and blood pressure and increase elasticity of the arteries.

Practical tips:
The high levels of polyunsaturated fats mean that walnuts spoil fairly quickly. Buy nuts with their shells on, if possible, store in the refrigerator, and consume quickly. Avoid buying chopped walnuts unless they are for immediate use—chopping speeds the oxidation of the nuts. Walnuts are best eaten raw as a snack, but they can also be added to cakes and other baked treats.

Walnut & seed bread

MAKES 2 LARGE LOAVES

3¾ cups whole-wheat flour

3⅓ cups white bread flour, plus extra for dusting

2 tablespoons sesame seeds

2 tablespoons sunflower seeds

2 tablespoons poppy seeds

1 cup whole walnuts, chopped

2 teaspoon salt

2 teaspoons active dry yeast

2 tablespoons olive oil or walnut oil

3 cups lukewarm water

1 tablespoon melted butter or oil, for greasing

METHOD

1　Mix together the flours, seeds, walnuts, salt, and yeast in a large bowl. Add the oil and water and stir well to form a soft dough. Invert the dough onto a lightly floured surface and knead well for 5–7 minutes, or until smooth and elastic.

2　Return the dough to the bowl, cover with a damp dish towel, and let stand in a warm place for 1–1½ hours to rise, or until the dough has doubled in size. Invert the dough onto a lightly floured surface and knead again for 1 minute.

3　Grease two 9-inch loaf pans with the butter. Divide the dough in half. Shape one piece to the length of the pan and three times the width. Fold the dough in three lengthwise and place in one of the pans with the seam underneath. Repeat with the other piece of dough.

4　Cover and put in a warm place for about 30 minutes, or until the bread is well risen.

5　Meanwhile, preheat the oven to 450°F. Bake in the center of the preheated oven for 25–30 minutes, or until golden brown. If the loaves are getting too brown during cooking, reduce the temperature to 425°F. Transfer to a wire rack to cool.

48

**MAJOR NUTRIENTS PER
¼ CUP/1¼ OZ. BRAZIL NUTS**

Calories	197
Total fat	19.9 g
Protein	4.3 g
Carbohydrate	3.7 g
Fiber	2.3 g
Vitamin E	1.7 mcg
Calcium	48 mg
Potassium	198 mg
Magnesium	113 mg
Zinc	1.2 mg
Selenium	575 mcg

Did you know?

Brazil nuts are not actually nuts, but seeds that are enclosed in a hard fruit. The trees grow wild in the Amazon rain forests of Brazil and are rarely successfully cultivated.

Brazil nuts

One of the richest food sources of the antioxidant mineral selenium, Brazil nuts are also a good source of calcium and magnesium for healthy bones.

Brazil nuts have a high total fat content. Much of this is monounsaturated, but there is also a reasonable amount of polyunsaturates and high content of omega-6 linoleic acid, one of the essential fats. When cooked at high temperatures, these fats oxidize and are no longer healthy, so Brazil nuts are best eaten raw. The nut has an extremely high content of the mineral selenium and, on average, just one to two nuts can provide a whole day's recommended intake. Selenium is vital for the healthy function of internal organs, such as the liver, kidneys, and pancreas. Brazil nuts are also a good source of magnesium and calcium.

• Extremely rich in selenium, a mineral often lacking in modern diets.
• High magnesium content protects heart and bones.
• A good source of vitamin E for healthy skin and healing.

Practical tips:
Keep unshelled nuts in a cool, dry, dark place for up to six months. Shelled nuts should be stored in the refrigerator and consumed within a few weeks because their high fat content means they spoil quickly. They are best eaten raw.

Trail mix

MAKES 12 SERVINGS

⅔ cup chopped dried apricots

½ cup dried cranberries

¾ cup roasted cashew nuts

⅔ cup shelled hazelnuts

⅔ cup shelled Brazil nuts, halved

¾ cup slivered almonds

¼ cup toasted pumpkin seeds

¼ cup sunflower seeds

¼ cup toasted pine nuts

METHOD

1 Place all the ingredients in an airtight container, close the lid, and shake several times. Shake the container before each opening, then reseal. This mix will stay fresh for up to two weeks if tightly sealed after each opening.

Coconut oil

Cooking with coconut oil is a simple way to reduce your exposure to the aging free radicals that are produced when roasting, frying, and baking.

**MAJOR NUTRIENTS PER
1 TABLESPOON COCONUT OIL**

Calories	129
Total fat	15 g
Lauric acid	6.69 g
Caprylic acid	1.125 g
Myristic acid	2.5 g
Omega-6 oils	270 mg
Omega-9 oils	870 mg
Protein	**Trace**
Carbohydrate	**Trace**
Fiber	**Trace**

Whenever we cook with oil, the heat causes damage to the oil's fat molecules, which has a knock-on effect when ingested. The free radicals produced can damage tissues and make us more susceptible to cancer, heart disease, and osteoporosis. Of all the saturated fats, coconut oil is the least prone to damage by heat, light, and oxygen, and can be heated to temperatures as high as 375°F. Coconut oil contains about 60 percent medium-chain triglycerides (MCTs), plant-based oils that raise metabolism and cannot be stored as fat in our bodies.

- The fats in coconut oil help renew the lining of the digestive tract, ensuring good digestion.
- Regular consumption has been shown to assist thyroid function and regulate metabolism and mood.

Practical tips:
Coconut oil, which becomes a clear liquid when heated, can be used in all kinds of cooking and doesn't retain any of the coconut flavor from the flesh. It does behave differently from other oils, however, so a little experimentation may be necessary. Choose an unprocessed variety, and avoid any that have been hydrogenated or contain preservatives.

Thai green curry

SERVES 4

2 tablespoons coconut oil

2 tablespoons Thai green curry paste

1 pound skinless, boneless chicken breasts, cut into cubes

2 kaffir lime leaves, coarsely torn

1 lemongrass stalk, finely chopped

1 cup canned coconut milk

16 baby eggplants, halved

2 tablespoons Thai fish sauce

fresh Thai basil sprigs and thinly sliced kaffir lime leaves, to garnish

METHOD

1 Heat a large wok or skillet over medium heat. Add the oil and heat for 30 seconds. Add the Thai curry paste and stir-fry briefly until all the aromas are released.

2 Add the chicken, lime leaves, and lemon grass and stir-fry for 3–4 minutes, until the meat is beginning to brown. Add the coconut milk and eggplants and simmer gently for 8–10 minutes, or until tender.

3 Stir in the fish sauce and serve immediately, garnished with Thai basil sprigs and lime leaves.

Olive oil

Well known for being high in heart-protective monounsaturates, virgin olive oils also contain a range of antioxidant plant compounds and vitamin E.

The main type of fat in olive oil is monounsaturated, which helps prevent cholesterol from being deposited on artery walls and, therefore, helps protect us from cardiovascular disease and strokes. In addition, early pressings of the olives (as in extra virgin olive oil, particularly "cold pressed" oil) produce an oil that is rich in beneficial plant compounds. These can protect against cancer and high blood pressure, and they can lower cholesterol and the compound oleocanthal, an anti-inflammatory with similar action to ibuprofen. Finally, olive oil is a good source of vitamin E.

- Helps improve blood cholesterol profile and protect us from cardiovascular disease.
- Rich in polyphenols to protect against colon and other cancers.
- Can help prevent *H. pylori*, which can lead to stomach ulcers.
- Antibacterial and antioxidant.

Practical tips:

Olive oil should be stored in the dark and used within two months of opening. When buying olive oil, choose a store that keeps it in dimly lit conditions and has high turnover. For the full benefit of olive oil, eat it cold in salad dressings or drizzled on bread or vegetables. Don't use extra virgin olive oil for cooking at high temperatures or the beneficial chemicals will be destroyed.

MAJOR NUTRIENTS PER 1 TABLESPOON OLIVE OIL

Calories	130
Total fat	15 g
Protein	Trace
Carbohydrate	Trace
Fiber	Trace
Vitamin C	Trace
Potassium	Trace
Lycopene	Trace
Lutein/Zeaxanthin	Trace

Did you know?

Light destroys many of the disease-fighting compounds in olive oil; after a year, oils stored in clear bottles under store lighting have shown at least a 30 percent decrease in antioxidants.

Lemon-infused olive oil

MAKES 1 CUP

zest of 1 lemon
1 whole lemon
2 teaspoon multicolored peppercorns
1 cup olive oil

METHOD

1 Cut the lemon zest into thin strips, making sure you omit the white pith. Thinly slice the other lemon. Crush the peppercorns in a mortar with a pestle.

2 Put the lemon zest, lemon slices, peppercorns, and oil in a heatproof bowl set over a saucepan of gently simmering water and heat for 1 hour. Make sure that you add extra water to the saucepan, when necessary, so the pan doesn't become dry.

3 Remove from the heat, let cool, then strain the lemon-infused oil through cheesecloth into a clean jar. Cover and store in the refrigerator. Alternatively, leave the lemon zest and peppercorns in the jar and store in the refrigerator, and then strain before using. Brush over white fish fillets or chicken breasts before cooking for a fresh, zesty flavor.